The Education Sect
The British Psychologic

25th Vernon-Wall Lecture

Self-concept theory, measurement and research into practice: The role of self-concept in educational psychology

Herbert W. Marsh
Oxford University

The 25th Vernon-Wall Lecture
presented at the
Annual Meeting of the Education Section of
The British Psychological Society

*

Durham University – 2005

Author note: This paper was the basis of my 2005 Vernon-Wall Keynote Address to the Educational Psychology section of the British Psychological Society at Durham University. Requests for further information about this investigation should be sent to Professor Herbert W. Marsh, Department of Educational Studies, University of Oxford, 15 Norham Gardens, Oxford, OX2 6PY. E-mail: herb.marsh@edstud.ox.ac.uk.

Contents

Self-concept theory, measurement and research into practice: The role of self-concept in educational psychology

Herbert W. Marsh
Oxford University

Self-concept enhancement is a major goal in many fields including education, child development, health, sport/exercise sciences, social services, organisational settings, and management. Self-concept is a multidimensional hierarchical construct with highly differentiated components such as academic, social, physical and emotional self-concepts in addition to a global self-concept component. Self-concept is also an important mediating factor that facilitates the attainment of other desirable outcomes. In education, for example, a positive academic self-concept is both a highly desirable goal and a means of facilitating subsequent academic accomplishments. However, the benefits of feeling positively about oneself in relation to choice, planning, persistence and subsequent accomplishments, transcend traditional disciplinary and cultural barriers. My purpose here is to provide an overview of my self-concept research in which I address diverse theoretical and methodological issues with practical implications for research, policy and practice such as:

- *Does a positive self-concept 'cause' better school performance or is it the other way around?*
- *Why do self-concepts decline for:*
  - *gifted students who attend selective schools?*
  - *learning disabled students in regular classrooms?*
- *Are multiple dimensions of self-concept more distinct than multiple intelligences?*
- *Why do people think of themselves as 'math' persons or 'verbal' persons?*
- *Can children as young as 5 or 6 distinguish between multiple dimensions of self-concept?*
- *How different are the self-concepts of bullies and victims?*
- *Does a positive physical self-concept lead to health-related physical activity?*
- *Do self-concept models hold up cross-nationally and cross-culturally?*
- *How do self-concepts of elite swimmers from 30 countries contribute to winning gold medals?*
- *How did the fall of the Berlin Wall and the resumption of Chinese control of Hong Kong influence self-concepts?*

Herbert W. Marsh

Significance of self-concept

Nathaniel Branden (1994, p.xv), an eminent philosopher and psychologist, attests to the significance of the self-concept/self-esteem construct and outcomes that are mediated by it, stating that:

> *I cannot think of a single psychological problem – from anxiety to depression, to under-achievement at school or at work, to fear of intimacy, happiness or success, to alcohol or drug abuse, to spouse battering or child molestation, to co-dependency and sexual disorders, to passivity and chronic aimlessness, to suicide and crimes of violence – that is not traceable, at least in part, to the problem of deficient self-esteem.*

As illustrated dramatically by Branden, self-concept research is highly relevant to important individual and societal problems that stem from low self-concept. At the heart of my research programme is this universal importance and multidisciplinary appeal of self-concept as one of the most important constructs in the social sciences. This importance of self-concept and related constructs is highlighted by the regularity/consistency with which self-concept enhancement is identified as a major focus of concern in diverse settings, including education, child development, mental and physical health, social services, industry, and sport/exercise. Educational policy statements throughout the world list self-concept enhancement as a central goal of education. For example, in their model of effective schools, Brookover and Lezotte (1979) emphasised that maximising academic self-concept, self-reliance, and academic achievement should be major outcome goals of schooling. Self-concept is also an important mediating factor that facilitates the attainment of other desirable psychological and behavioural outcomes. The need to think and feel positively about oneself, and the likely benefits of these positive cognitions on choice, planning, and subsequent accomplishments transcend traditional disciplinary barriers, and are central to goals in many social policy areas.

Self-concept is also one of the oldest, most important, most controversial and most widely studied constructs in the social sciences. Despite this long history, advances in theory, research and measurement of self-concept were slow – particularly during the heyday of behaviourism. It is only in the last three decades that there has been a resurgence in self-concept research. Even now, although many thousands of studies have examined self-concept, few researchers have published a significant number of studies or have conducted self-concept research over an extended period. In many studies, the major focus is on some other construct (e.g. academic achievement, school persistence, bullying, and drug problems) and a measure of self-concept is included because of its assumed relevance. Reviews of this early research (e.g. Byrne, 1984; Burns, 1982; Shavelson *et al.*, 1976; Wells & Marwell, 1976; Wylie, 1974, 1979) emphasised weak theoretical bases, poor quality of measurement instruments, methodological shortcomings, and a lack of consistent findings. Similar observations led Hattie (1992) to describe this period as one of 'dustbowl empiricism' in which the predominant research design in self-concept studies was to 'throw it in and see what happens.'

In contrast, the period since the 1980s has seen a renaissance of self-concept research that has been exciting to be part of. Studies during this modern era have made important advances in theory, measurement, and research. Particularly in educational psychology, but in other disciplines as well, much of this progress is due to a stimulating new interplay between theory, research, measurement and practice. Building on the work of Shavelson *et al.* (1976), my colleagues and I developed and refined this important theoretical model of self-concept (Marsh, Byrne & Shavelson, 1988; Marsh & Shavelson, 1985; Shavelson, *et al.*, 1976; Shavelson & Marsh, 1986; also see Marsh & Hattie, 1996) and developed a construct validity approach (see Marsh, 1990b, 1990c, 1993a). We argued that the determination of theoretically consistent and distinguishable domains of self-concept should be prerequisite to the study of how self-concept is related to other variables. A critical starting point for my research in this area was the development of psychometrically sound instruments with a strong theoretical basis. Theory building and instrument construction are inexorably intertwined, such that each will suffer if the two are separated. Using the Shavelson *et al.* model as a 'blueprint,' I developed the set of Self Description Questionnaires (SDQ) instruments for preadolescents (SDQI), adolescents (SDQII), and late-adolescents and young adults (SDQIII). Subsequent reviews of this early research (Byrne, 1984; Hattie, 1992; Marsh & Shavelson, 1985; Marsh, 1990c, 1993a) supported the multifaceted structure of self-concept and demonstrated that self-concept cannot be adequately understood if its multidimensionality is ignored. In her influential review of all major self-concept instruments commissioned by the American Psychological Association, Byrne concluded that each of the three SDQ instruments were among the best available for their respective age groups. For example, in her review of the SDQI, she noted that:

> *The SDQ-I is clearly the most validated self-concept instrument available. ... For more than a decade, it has been the target of a well-planned research strategy to firmly establish its construct validity, as well as its other psychometric properties. In using the SDQ-I, researchers, clinicians, counsellors, and others interested in the welfare of preadolescent children can feel confident in the validity of interpretation based on responses to its multidimensionally sensitive items* (p.117).

The Shavelson et al. and Marsh/Shavelson theoretical models of self-concept

The Shavelson et al. model

The Shavelson et al. (1976) review and theoretical model of self-concept was a landmark in the renaissance of self-concept research. Shavelson et al. (1976) noted important deficiencies in self-concept research, concluding that 'it appears that self-concept research has addressed itself to substantive problems before problems of definition, measurement, and interpretation have been resolved' (p.470). However, unlike many other pessimistic reviews of the state of self-concept research, Shavelson et al. (1976) emphasised 'our approach is constructive in that we (a) develop a definition of self-concept from existing definitions, (b) review some steps in validating a construct interpretation of a test score, and (c) apply these steps in examining five popularly used self-concept instruments' (p.470).

Shavelson et al. (1976) began their review by developing a theoretical definition of self-concept. An ideal definition, they emphasised, consists of the nomological network containing within-network and between-network components. The within-network portion of the network pertains to specific features of the construct – its components, structure, and attributes and theoretical statements relating these features. The between-network portion of the definition locates the construct in a broader conceptual space, indicating how self-concept is related to other constructs. Thus, for example, dividing self-concept into academic, social and physical components is a within-network proposition whereas a related between-network proposition is that academic self-concept is more strongly related to academic achievement than are physical and social self-concepts.

Shavelson et al. (1976), integrating features from many definitions of self-concept, defined self-concept to be a person's self-perceptions that are formed through experience with and interpretations of one's environment. They are influenced especially by evaluations by significant others, reinforcements, and attributions for one's own behaviour. Shavelson et al. (1976) emphasised that self-concept is not an entity within the person, but a hypothetical construct that is potentially useful in explaining and predicting how a person acts. These self-perceptions influence the way one acts and these acts in turn influence one's self-perceptions. Consistently with this perspective, Shavelson et al. (1976) noted that self-concept is important as both an outcome and as a mediating variable that helps to explain other outcomes. Thus, for example, academic self-concept may be an important outcome that is influenced by an experimental intervention. Alternatively, academic self-concept may mediate the influence of an academic intervention that is designed to enhance academic achievement. In this second example, the intervention effect on academic achievement is due at least in part to the effect of the intervention on academic self-concept, which in turn influences academic achievement. In this sense, the effect of the intervention on academic achievement is facilitated by the effect of the intervention on academic self-concept even though the enhancement of academic self-concept may not be the main aim of the study.

Shavelson et al. (1976) identified seven features that were critical to their definition of the self-concept construct:

1. It is organised or structured, in that people categorise the vast amount of information they have about themselves and relate these categories to one another.

2. It is multidimensional, and the particular dimensions reflect a self-referent cate-

gory system adopted by a particular individual and/or shared by a group.

3. It is hierarchical, with perceptions of personal behaviour in specific situations at the base of the hierarchy, inferences about self in broader domains (e.g. social, physical, and academic) at the middle of the hierarchy, and a global, general self-concept at the apex. Shavelson *et al.* (1976) likened this structure to a hierarchical representation of intellectual abilities with Spearman's 'g' (see Vernon, 1950) at the apex.

4. The hierarchical general self-concept – the apex of the hierarchy – is stable, but as one descends the hierarchy, self-concept becomes increasingly situation specific and, as a consequence, less stable. There are reciprocal relations between self-concept at each level in that self-perceptions at the base of the hierarchy may be attenuated by conceptualisations at higher levels, and changes in general self-concept may require changes in many situation-specific instances.

5. Self-concept becomes increasingly multidimensional as the individual moves from infancy to adulthood.

6. Self-concept has both a descriptive and an evaluative aspect such that individuals may describe themselves ('I am happy') and evaluate themselves ('I do well in mathematics'). Evaluations can be made against some absolute ideal (the five minute mile), a personal, internal standard (a personal best), a relative standard based on comparisons with peers, or the expectations of significant others. Individuals may differentially weight specific dimensions.

7. Self-concept can be differentiated from other constructs. Thus, for example, academic and physical self-concepts can be differentiated from related constructs such as academic achievement and physical fitness respectively.

Shavelson *et al.* (1976) also presented one possible representation of this hierarchical model (see Figure 1 overleaf) in which general-self appeared at the apex and was divided into academic and non-academic self-concepts at the next level. Academic self-concept was further divided into self-concepts in particular subject areas (e.g. mathematics, English, etc.). Non-academic self-concept was divided into three areas: social self-concept, which was subdivided into relations with peers and with significant others; emotional self-concept; and physical self-concept, which was subdivided into physical ability and physical appearance. Further levels of division were hypothesised for each of these specific self-concepts so that at the base of the hierarchy self-concepts were of limited generality, quite specific, and more closely related to actual behaviour. This model posits a structure of self-concept that resembles British psychologists' hierarchical model of intellectual abilities (Vernon, 1950) where general ability (like Spearman's 'g') was at the apex. The figure turned out to be so important, in part, because it provided a blueprint for a new generation of multidimensional self-concept instruments that have had an important influence on the field.

Shavelson *et al.* (1976) systematically applied the construct validity approach to self-concept research in a classic review that had a profound influence on the field. Shavelson *et al.* argued that the starting point of a construct validity approach is a definition of the construct to be evaluated which provides a blueprint for constructing self-concept instruments, for designing within-network studies of the proposed structure of self-concept, for testing between-network hypotheses about relations with other constructs, and, eventually, rejecting and revising the original construct definition.

Self Description Questionnaires

Shavelson *et al.* used his approach to evaluate five self-concept instruments then popular: Brookover's Self-concept of Ability Scale; Coopersmith's Self-Esteem Inventory;

Figure 1: Pictorial representation of the multidimensional, hierarchical model of self–concept posited by Shavelson, Hubner and Stanton (1976; Marsh & Shavelson, 1985).

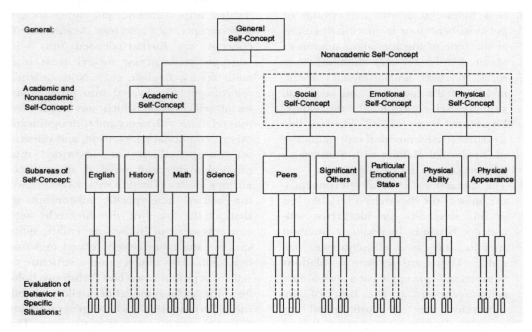

The box consisting of dashed lines around the non-academic self-concept factors is used to distinguish these from the academic self-concept factors, but does not imply that there is a single higher-order non-academic factor, as is hypothesised for the academic factors. The unlabelled boxes in the bottom of the hierarchy are used to show that the model posits additional levels in the hierarchy and even more domain-specific components of self-concept than those that are explicitly presented (e.g. math self-concept might be broken into different mathematical topics such as algebra, trigonometry, or calculus, and each of these could be further subdivided into specific components relevant to each of the mathematical subjects). Reprinted with permission from Shavelson *et al.* (1976, p.413).

Gordon's How I See Myself Scale; the Piers-Harris Children's Self-Concept Scale; Sear's Self-concept Inventory. However, based on this review, there was only modest support for their hypothesised domains and none of these five instruments was able to differentiate among even the broad academic, social, and physical domains. Although heuristic, there was little or no empirical support for the Shavelson *et al.* model at the time it was proposed. So strong was resistance to the multidimensional aspect of the model in particular that major researchers of that period (e.g. Coopersmith, 1967; Marx & Winne, 1978) argued that self-concept was either a unidimensional construct or that the facets of self-concept were dominated so heavily by a general factor that they could not be differentiated adequately. Coopersmith, on the basis of preliminary research with his Self-Esteem Inventory, argued that 'preadolescent children make little distinction about their worthiness in different areas of experience or, if such distinctions are made, they are made within the context of the over-all, general appraisal of worthiness that children have already made' (p.6). Based on empirical research with three leading self-concept instruments of the period Marx and Winne concluded that 'self-concept seems more of a unitary concept than one broken into distinct subparts or facets' (p.900). As recently as 1984 Byrne (1984, pp.449–450) noted that: 'Many consider this inability to attain discriminant validity among the dimensions of SC to be one of the major complexities facing SC researchers today.' In retrospect – as clearly articulated by Shavelson *et al.* (1976) – the renaissance of self-concept research was floundering due to the lack of a solid basis of measurement to support it.

In order to address these concerns, I developed SDQ instruments for pre-adolescent primary school students (SDQI), adolescent high school students (SDQII), and late adolescents and young adults (SDQIII). Reviews of subsequent SDQ research (Byrne, 1984; Hattie, 1992; Marsh & Shavelson, 1985; Marsh, 1990c, 1993a) supported the multidimensional structure of self-concept and demonstrated that self-concept cannot be adequately understood if its multidimensionality is ignored. The set of three SDQ instruments has provided particularly strong tests of the Shavelson *et al.* model, and have been evaluated to be among the best multidimensional instruments in terms of psychometric properties and construct validation research (Hattie, 1992; Byrne, 1984; Boyle, 1994; Wylie, 1989). Here I review initial research leading to development of the SDQ instruments and the subsequent refinement of the original Shavelson model based on this SDQ research (see overviews by Marsh, 1990a, 1993a).

The initial focus of SDQ research was on the within-network concerns. I reasoned that the determination of whether theoretically consistent and distinguishable dimensions of self-concept existed, and their content and structure, should be prerequisite to the study of how these dimensions, or overall self-concept, are related to other variables. In adopting such an approach, I rejected atheoretical and purely empirical approaches to developing and refining measurement instruments. Instead, I took an explicit theoretical model as my starting point for instrument construction, and I used empirical results to support, refute or revise the instrument *and* the theory upon which it is based. In applying this approach, I judged the Shavelson *et al.* (1976) model to be the best available theoretical model of self-concept. Implicit in my approach is the presumption that theory building and instrument construction are inexorably intertwined, and that each will suffer if the two are separated. In this sense I based the SDQ instruments on a strong empirical foundation and a good theoretical model. Consistently with this approach, SDQ research provided support for the Shavelson *et al.* (1976) model, but also led to its subsequent revision.

SDQ research began by critically evaluating the within-network components of the Shavelson *et al.* model and the psychometric properties of the SDQ instruments. SDQ scales were posited on the basis of the Shavelson *et al.* (1976) model, item pools were constructed for each scale, and factor analyses and item analyses were used to select and refine the items eventually used to represent each scale. The internal consistency of the scales from the three SDQ instruments was good – typically in the 0.80s and 0.90s. The stability of SDQ responses was also good, particularly for older children. For example, the stability of SDQIII scales measured on four occasions varied from a median of 0.87 for a one-month interval to a median of $r = 0.74$ for intervals of 18 months or longer. Dozens of factor analyses by diverse samples differing in gender, age, country, and language have consistently identified the factors that each SDQ instrument is designed to measure. Marsh (1989) summarised factor analyses of more than 12,000 sets of responses from the normative archives of the three SDQ instruments. In addition to clearly identifying all of the factors that each of the three SDQ instruments is designed to measure, the results indicate that the domains of self-concept are remarkably distinct (median rs among the SDQ scales vary between 0.1 and 0.2 for the three SDQ instruments.

Whereas SDQ results provided strong support for the Shavelson *et al.* (1976) model and the multidimensionality of self-concept, they also posed some complications. The strong hierarchical structure posited by Shavelson *et al.* (1976) required self-concepts to be substantially correlated, but the small sizes of correlations actually observed implied that any hierarchical structure of the self-concept responses must be much weaker than anticipated. More specifically, in the Shavelson *et al.* (1976) model math and verbal self-concepts were assumed to be correlated substantially so that they could be described in terms of a single higher-order academic self-concept. Factor analyses, however, resulted in correlations between verbal and math self-concepts that were close to zero. Complications such as these led to the Marsh/Shavelson revision (Marsh *et al.*, 1988; Marsh & Shavelson, 1985; Marsh, 1990c) of the original Shavelson *et al.* (1976) model.

The Marsh/Shavelson model

The Shavelson *et al.* model posits that self-concept is hierarchically ordered as well as being multidimensional. We (Marsh & Hocevar, 1985; Marsh & Shavelson, 1985) applied the then recent advances in confirmatory factor analysis (CFA) to test first order and higher-order structures in responses to the SDQI by students in Grades 2–5. In preliminary first-order models the correlations among the SDQI factors were estimated, but no special assumptions about the pattern of correlations were made. However, both the Shavelson *et al.* (1976) model and the design of the SDQI assume that there is a systematic hierarchical ordering of the domains of self-concept which underlie these correlations among first-order factors. For example, the SDQI measures four non-academic domains and three academic domains of self-concept so that one reasonable hypothesis would be that the seven first-order factors would form two second-order factors, a finding which would be consistent with the Shavelson *et al.* (1976) model.

The hierarchical structure of self-concept was examined by comparing several competing models. In one model, a single, general self-concept factor was proposed to explain the relationships among the first-order factors, but this model was unable to fit the data very well at any grade level. In a second model, two second-order factors were proposed – one defined by the four non-academic factors and one defined by the three academic factors. This model fitted the data better than the first model, but still was not adequate. The final model took into account previous research showing verbal and math self-concepts to be nearly uncorrelated. Two second-order academic factors – math/academic and verbal/academic self-concepts, and a second-order non-academic factor were found. This model fitted the data significantly better than any other model for each of the four years in school. These results were consistent with Shavelson *et al.*'s (1976) assumption that self-concept is hierarchically ordered, but the particular form of this higher-order structure was more complicated than originally proposed. This led to the Marsh/Shavelson revision of the Shavelson *et al.* (1976) model that differs from the original model primarily in that there are two higher-order academic factors – math/academic and verbal/academic – instead of just one. A similar model was also supported – particularly the need for two separate higher-order academic factors – by Marsh (1987) with responses by late-adolescents to the SDQIII.

More generally, this research showed that the hierarchy of self-concept factors was much weaker than originally proposed. Correlations among the first-order factors were so small (median rs between 0.1 and 0.2 for the three SDQ instruments) that a higher-order factor was unable to explain much variance in the first-order factors. This was a truly remarkable finding in the context of the zeitgeist of only a decade earlier, when researchers concluded that self-concept was unidimensional. As emphasised by Marsh and Hattie (1996) this astonishing shift in thinking about the self-concept construct from a unidimensional to a multidimensional perspective, was brought about by the interplay between theory, measurement, and the availability of stronger statistical analyses.

Marsh *et al.* (1988) extended tests of the revised Marsh/Shavelson model by evaluating responses to the verbal, math, and general school scales from three different self-concept instruments. Hierarchical CFA was again employed and the critical test was whether correlations among these nine first-order factors could be adequately explained by a single higher-order factor as posited in the original Shavelson *et al.* (1976) model or whether two higher-order factors as posited in the Marsh/Shavelson revision were required (see Figure 2). The results showed conclusively that the Marsh/Shavelson revised model was superior. All three verbal self-concept scales were nearly uncorrelated with each of the three math self-concept scales and in the hierarchical model, the verbal/academic and math/academic higher-order factors were uncorrelated. These results provided strong support for the generality of earlier SDQ research and for the revised model.

Marsh *et al.* (1988) critically evaluated the Marsh/Shavelson model. Support for this revised model was based primarily on demonstrating apparent problems with the original Shavelson *et al.* (1976) model. Whereas there was strong evidence that a single higher-order academic component was insufficient, there was not strong support that just two higher-order academic factors were sufficient. Part of the problem, they argued, was that the revised model had not been presented in sufficient detail. To remedy this problem, they provided a more detailed development of the academic self-concept structure in the revised model (Figure 2 overleaf) and how it differs from the academic portion of the original Shavelson *et al.* (1976) model. The specific academic domains in Figure 2 were selected to broadly reflect core school subjects in a typical academic curriculum and the subject areas were roughly ordered from relatively pure measures of the math/academic component to relatively pure measures of the verbal/ academic component. In order to evaluated this model it was necessary to design new academic self-concept instruments that included a wider variety of specific academic self-concept domains.

Academic Self-Description Questionnaires (ASDQ)

Marsh (1990c) designed the Academic Self Description Questionnaire (ASDQ) I and II for elementary and high school students.

Figure 2: The academic portion of Shavelson, Hubner and Stanton's (1976) original model (see academic component of Figure 1) and an elaboration of Marsh and Shavelson's (1985) revision that includes a wider variety of specific academic facets. (S.C. = self-concept.).

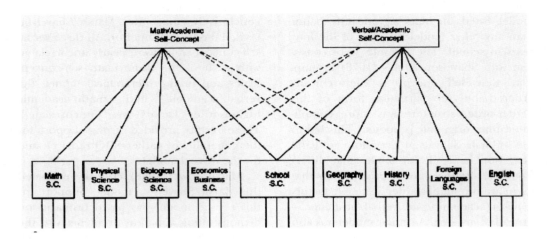

Reprinted with permission from Marsh, H.W., Byrne, B.M. & Shavelson, R. (1988). A multifaceted academic self-concept: Its hierarchical structure and its relation to academic achievement. *Journal of Educational Psychology, 80,* 366–380.

In consultation with school administrators 'core' subjects like those in Figure 2 and other 'non-core' school subjects taken by all students were determined, and a separate 6-item self-concept scale was constructed for each subject. The ASDQI and ASDQII respectively consist of 12 scales (seven core and five non-core) and 15 (nine core and six non-core) scales. For each scale, the wording of the six items is parallel except for the particular subject area. For example, on the ASDQII one of the six items is 'I learn things quickly in [a specific subject area, e.g. mathematics]' and students responded to this item on a six-category true/false response scale like that used on the SDQII. In addition, there is a general school scale in which the term 'most school subjects' is substituted for the specific academic subjects.

First-order factor analyses

Preliminary exploratory factor analyses were conducted on ASDQI and ASDQII responses. For ASDQI responses, all 13 self-concept scales that the instrument was designed to measure were identified and the reliability estimates for each scale varied from 0.88 to 0.94. For ASDQII responses, 16 reasonably well defined factors were identified by exploratory factor analyses and reliability estimates for the 16 scales varied from 0.88 to 0.95. However, the English language and English literature factors were not well differentiated even though all the remaining factors corresponded unambiguously to one of the scales the instrument was designed to measure. A 15-factor solution resulted in a well-defined solution in which variables from the two English scales loaded on the same factor. CFA results also resulted in well-defined solutions that fitted the data well. These results demonstrated that students are remarkably effective in distinguishing among a diverse set of academic self-concepts.

Correlations among the 13 ASDQI factors were all positive, varying from 0.04 (physical education and music) to 0.91 (science and social studies). The general

school factor was substantially more correlated with the core academic factors (0.26 to 0.73; median = 0.62) than with the other factors (0.18 to 0.34; median = 0.30). Physical education was substantially correlated with health (0.73) but not substantially correlated with any other scales, suggesting that a second-order physical education factor may be necessary. The art, music, and religion factors were not substantially correlated with any other scales, suggesting that they could not be well explained by second-order factors.

The correlations among the 16 ASDQII factors varied from −0.03 (physical education and music) to 0.98 (English language and English literature). The extremely high correlation between the two English scales suggests that students did not distinguish between English language and literature. The general school factor was substantially more correlated with the core academic factors (0.40 to 0.75; median = 0.59) than with the other factors (0.21 to 0.49; median = 0.29). Physical education was substantially correlated with health (0.55) but not substantially correlated with any other factors, suggesting that a second-order physical education factor may be necessary. Art was substantially correlated with industrial arts, and to a lesser extent, music and religion, but not to other factors, suggesting that a second-order art factor may be necessary.

Higher-order factor analyses

For both the ASDQI and ASDQII studies, the initial analyses were conducted on the set of core academic factors selected to represent those in Figure 2. A model positing just one (general academic) higher-order factor, as predicted, was not able to fit the data in either study. The fit of the model with two higher-order factors (verbal/ academic and math/academic) was reasonably good and clearly better than the one-factor model. Freeing additional parameters improved the fit somewhat, but the parameter estimates still clearly supported the two-higher-order-factor model. However, in all the models much of the reliable variance in the first-order factors could not be explained in terms of the higher-order factors.

Subsequent analyses were conducted on the entire set of core and non-core ASDQ scales for each instrument. These additional first-order factors were included specifically to test the limits of the generality of the Marsh/Shavelson model. Consistent with expectations, neither one- nor two-higher-order-factor models were able to adequately explain relations among the larger sets of first-order factors. In each case, at least two additional higher-order factors – defined substantially by the physical education and art first-order factors – were required. Even these more complicated four-higher-order-factor models were only moderately successful in fitting the data and again, much of the variance in first-order factors could not be explained in terms of the higher-order factors. It was also important to note that in all the different analyses, the first-order general school factor loaded substantially on the second-order math/academic and second-order verbal/academic factors, but was nearly unrelated to second-order factors defined by the remaining non-core scales.

Summary and implications of the multifaceted structure of self-concept

The original Shavelson *et al.* model of self-concept hypothesised that self-concepts in specific school subjects could be explained in terms of a single higher-order dimension of academic self-concept. A growing body of research subsequently demonstrated that at least two higher-order academic factors – math/academic and verbal/academic – were required; this led to the Marsh/ Shavelson revision. The ASDQ studies extended this research by examining a greater diversity of academic self-concepts domains than hereto-fore considered and provided reasonable support for the Marsh/Shavelson model when consideration was limited to core academic factors like those in Figure 2. It is important to emphasise, however, that much of the variance in many of the first-order factors was not explained by the higher-order factors (i.e. residual variances of the first-order factors were large). Whereas the two higher-order factors were able to explain correlations among the first-order factors with reasonable accuracy, the actual levels of self-concept on many of the first-order factors cannot be accurately inferred from the two higher-order factors. Thus, support for the theoretical model should not be interpreted to mean that academic self-concepts in subjects like computer studies, handwriting, geography, history, foreign languages, and commerce can be well-represented by more general components of academic self-concept. The results show quite the opposite.

Because previous research has not considered such a diversity of academic self-concepts, a substantively important question is whether or not students differentiate among self-concepts associated with specific school subjects. Perhaps the most remarkable finding is that students can differentiate self-concepts in so many different school subjects to a much greater extent than had been previously recognised. If researchers are specifically interested in self-concepts in particular academic subjects, then they should measure self-concepts with scales specific to those subjects in addition to, perhaps, more general academic self-concept scales. The design of the ASDQ instruments – if not the specific scales – provides researchers with an easy way to measure academic self-concept in different school subjects that is applicable across most educational settings.

Unidimensional versus multidimensional perspectives

It follows naturally from the clear support for the multidimensionality of self-concept that theory, research, applied practice and policy should adopt a multidimensional perspective. However, particularly in applied research, there has been a heavy reliance on use of general self-esteem (typically using some variation of the Rosenberg, 1965, instrument) as the only measure of self-concept. Use of a single global scale is based, at least implicitly, on a unidimensional perspective. If the self-concept hierarchy was sufficiently strong, this unidimensional approach might represent an expedient compromise between a more appropriate multidimensional perspective and the desire to limit the number of items included on a survey in applied research. However, research showed that the self-concept hierarchy is weak – that relatively small amounts of variance in specific components of self-concept can be explained in terms of self-esteem. Whereas research in educational psychology has led the way in moving from older, unidimensional perspectives of self-concept to a newer, multidimensional perspective, acceptance of the multidimensional perspective has been slower in self-concept research more generally.

In self-concept research there continues to be an ongoing debate about the relative usefulness of unidimensional perspectives that emphasise a single, relatively unidimensional, global domain of self-concept (typically referred to as self-esteem) and multidimensional perspectives based on multiple, relatively distinct components of self-concept. For example, Suls (1993) noted the extreme divergence of claims in chapters written by Marsh (1993a) and Brown (1993) that appeared in his monograph, concluding, 'both Brown and Marsh, who cite strong support for their viewpoints, cannot be right; or, at minimum, a new inte-grative theory is needed to reconcile the two approaches' (p.x). Based particularly on research in educational settings, Marsh and Craven (1997, p.191) argued that:

> If the role of self-concept research is to better understand the complexity of self in different contexts, to predict a wide variety of behaviours, to provide outcome measures for diverse interventions, and to relate self-concept to other constructs, then the specific domains of self-concept are more useful than a general domain.

Historically, self-concept research was dominated by a unidimensional perspective in which self-concept was typically represented by a single score variously referred to as general self-concept, total self-concept, global self-worth, or self-esteem (here we treat these terms as synonymous; see Marsh, 1993a). As described earlier, Shavelson *et al.* (1976) developed a multidimensional, hierarchical model of self-concept and argued for a construct validity approach to the measurement of self-concept. Following from the Shavelson *et al.* (1976) review, self-concept researchers (e.g. Byrne, 1996b; Marsh & Hattie, 1996; Wylie, 1989) have routinely evaluated responses to self-concept instruments through the application of: (a) confirmatory factor analysis (CFA) to evaluate the structure of self-concept; (b) structural equation models (SEMs) to relate self-concept to other constructs; and (c) multitrait-multimethod (MTMM) analyses to establish the convergent and discriminant validity of self-concept responses. Early research based on the SDQ instruments provided strong support for the multidimensionality of self-concept responses (see review by Byrne, 1996a). In support of a multidimensional perspective, this research also showed that the proposed hierarchy was weak and that the specific components of self-concept (e.g. social, academic, physical, emotional) were highly differentiated (Marsh & Craven, 1997).

Multidimensional perspectives in different disciplines

In many psychological disciplines (e.g. education, sport, and development) this multidimensional perspective of self-concept is now widely accepted.

Educational psychology

Educational psychology provides particularly compelling support for the multidimensional perspective (Marsh, 1993a). In this area, many important academic outcomes (e.g. academic achievement, coursework selection) are substantially related to academic self-concept but relatively unrelated to self-esteem and non-academic components of self-concept (e.g. Byrne, 1996a; Marsh, 1993a; Marsh, Trautwein *et al.*, 2006). Thus, for example, Marsh (1992) demonstrated that relations between academic self-concepts in specific school subjects were substantially related to school grades in the matching school subjects (rs = 0.45 to 0.70; M r = 0.57), whereas self-esteem was nearly uncorrelated with any of the school grades.

Multitrait-multimethod analyses demonstrated that the agreement between multiple dimensions of self-concept and grades was highly specific to particular school subjects, but that the academic self-concept factors were much better differentiated (mean r = 0.33) than the corresponding set of school grades (mean r = 0.58). Causal ordering studies demonstrated that academic self-concept influences subsequent academic achievement, coursework selection, and accomplishments beyond what can be explained by prior academic achievement, whereas self-esteem has little or no influence. Marsh and Yeung (1997a, b) demonstrated that whereas self-concepts in school subjects and matching school grades were both substantially correlated, the specific components of academic self-concept predicted subsequent coursework

selection much better than school grades or more general components of self-concept.

This domain specificity of self-concept was also highlighted in a recent study of German high school students (Marsh, Trautwein *et al.*, 2006). Global self-esteem was nearly uncorrelated with each of nine academic outcomes (rs = −0.03 to 0.05) consisting of standardised test scores, school grades, and coursework selection in different school subjects, but there were large and systematic patterns of relations between math, German, and English self-concepts and corresponding outcomes. For example, math self-concept was substantially and positively related to math school grades (0.71), math standardised achievement test scores (0.59), and taking advanced math courses (0.51), but was nearly unrelated or even negatively related to English and German outcomes. Cross-cultural research from around the world (e.g. Marsh & Hau, 2004) demonstrated that math and verbal self-concept are nearly uncorrelated with each other even though both these academic self-concepts are substantially correlated with achievement in each of these areas and with global academic self-concept. In summary, self-esteem is not a particularly useful variable in predicting a variety of key constructs in educational psychology research

Sport psychology

Reflecting historical trends in self-concept research more generally, self-concept instruments used in early physical education and sport/exercise research focused on global self-esteem (Marsh, 1997, 2002). More recently, however, there has been a stronger emphasis on physical self-concept measures designed specifically for physical education, sport and exercise settings (Fox & Corbin, 1989; Marsh, 1997, 2002), providing clear evidence for their convergent and discriminant validity in relation to other self-concept domains (e.g. academic) and to sport/exercise outcome measures. This follows the more general trend in sport/exercise psychology research to develop sport/ exercise-specific instruments and to evaluate them within a construct validity framework (e.g. Gill *et al.*, 1988).

SDQ research provided good support for the construct validity of the physical ability and appearance scales that appear on the SDQ instruments (Marsh, 2002; Marsh & Peart, 1988), but left unanswered the important question as to whether physical self-concept is more differentiated than can be explained in terms of one (physical ability) or two (ability, appearance) physical scales. The Physical SDQ (PSDQ; Marsh, Richards *et al.*, 1994), developed to address this issue, comprises some SDQ scales (physical ability, physical appearance, and self-esteem), and factors derived from components of physical fitness (Marsh, 1993c) based on an extension of Fleishman's (1964) classic research on the structure of physical fitness. In research summarised by Marsh (1997, 2002), there is good support for internal consistency, short- and long-term test-retest stability, convergent and discriminant validity in relation to other physical self-concept instruments and to external validity criteria (reflecting body composition, physical activity, and other components of physical fitness). Hence, there now exists strong support for the multidimensional perspective of self-concept in sport/exercise psychology (Marsh, 1997, 2002).

Developmental psychology and focus on early childhood

For many educational, developmental, and psychological researchers, self-concepts are a 'cornerstone of both social and emotional development' in early childhood (Kagen, Moore & Bredekamp, 1995, p.18; also see Davis-Kean & Sandler, 2001; Marsh, Debus & Bornholt, 2005; Marsh, Ellis & Craven, 2002). It is argued that self-concepts develop early in childhood and that, once established, they are enduring (e.g. Eder & Mangelsdorf, 1997). The development of self-concept is, therefore, emphasised in many early childhood programmes (e.g.

Fantuzzo, McDermott *et al.*, 1996). However, there has been surprisingly little systematic research with young children. Davis-Kean and Sandler (2001) emphasised that early childhood programmes need a reliable basis for evaluating interventions to enhance children's self-concepts (see Fantuzzo, McDermott *et al.*, 1996). Currently available inventories for young children use a wide range of techniques, such as pictures, Q-sort, one-to-one interview, questionnaires, and puppets, often with limited success (Byrne, 1996b; Wylie, 1989).

We (Marsh, Debus & Bornholt, 2005) were asked to evaluate methodological approaches and empirical support for assessing the validity of young children's responses to self-concept instruments for the *Handbook of Developmental Psychology*. In a brief review of the research with older children, we argued that recent advances in the field had been due to the use of new self-concept instruments with sound theoretical and empirical bases, and to improved methodological and statistical approaches to data analysis. By way of analogy, we reasoned that advances in self-concept research with younger children also required corresponding improvements in age-appropriate instruments with an emphasis on the validation of responses. More specifically, in that chapter we: evaluated theoretical approaches and empirical support for self-reports by young children that differentiate among multiple dimensions of self-concept; evaluated approaches to construct validity of young children's responses; reviewed self-concept instruments for young children; and outlined the special issues that arise in the assessment of self-concepts for young children.

How young can we go? Our review of theoretical work (see Marsh, Debus & Bornholt, 2005) convinced us that self-concept was formed at a very young age, so that it should be possible to devise age-appropriate measures of self-concept for young children. However, there was limited empirical support for these optimistic expectations.

In seminal work we (Marsh, Craven & Debus, 1991; 1998) developed and replicated an Individualised Administration (IA) procedure for use with the SDQI-IA self-concept instrument. This procedure consists of an individual interview style of presentation. Results based on these two studies demonstrated a clearly defined factor structure based on responses by children between the ages of 5 and 8. Important results of these studies include: (a) the development of a sound self-concept measurement instrument for young children; (b) illuminating the structure of self-concept for young children, including ascertaining that young children do conceptualise a general self-concept; (c) the identification of age and gender differences typified for older students being extended to these very young children; and (d) clarification of pragmatic issues such as the length of instruments for young children.

Although it had typically been assumed that longer instruments (e.g. 64 items on the SDQI-IA) are inappropriate for young children aged 5 to 8, our results showed the opposite pattern. For items presented in random order, those near the end of the questionnaire were more effective than those at the beginning or middle of the instrument. It appears that young children learned to respond more appropriately to the items with practice so that items near the beginning of the instrument had the poorest psychometric properties. These results have important implications for research with young children, where it is typically assumed that researchers should limit themselves to very short instruments. Our research suggests quite the opposite and may explain in part why the psychometric properties of the SDQI-IA are so much better than those typically found with responses by young children.

Building on this work in her recently completed PhD thesis in special education, Tracey (Tracey, 2004; Tracey, Marsh & Craven, 2003; also Marsh, Tracey & Craven, 2006) demonstrated that self-concepts of young, academically disadvantaged students could also be effectively measured with this individualised administration procedure. This research was important because research prior to this study had not been able to demonstrate a well-defined factor structure for young children with special learning disadvantages. Hence, as appears to be the case with young children, the problems were due to limitations in instrument construction, methodology and appropriate statistical analyses rather than inherent limitations with this population of children with special needs.

Extending this individualised administration procedure even further, Marsh, Ellis and Craven (2002) conducted pilot research utilising the SDQ-IA with pre-school children aged 4 to 5. For this very young group, they found that some of the SDQI items could not be understood easily and some items were more appropriate for a schooling context rather than an early childhood setting. In a series of interviews with young children they attempted to develop suitable items. The final 38-item instrument (SDQ-P) was designed to measure six self-concept factors (physical, appearance, peers, parents, verbal, math). About half the items were from the original SDQI. Using an individual-interview procedure, young children ($N = 100$, aged 4.0 to 5.6 years) completed the SDQ-P and achievement tests. The psychometric properties were good in that the self-concept scales were reliable (ranging from 0.75 to 0.89; Md = 0.83), first and higher-order confirmatory factor models fitted the data well, and correlations among the scales were moderate (−0.03 to 0.73; Md = 0.29). Achievement test-scores correlated modestly with academic self-concept factors (rs 0.15 to 0.40), but were non-significantly or significantly negatively related to non-academic self-concept scales. Gender and age differences, although mostly small, were suggestive of developmental trends that are consistent with results based on responses with older children. The results showed that very young children do distinguish between multiple dimensions of self-concept at a younger age than suggested by previous research. Verbal and math self-concepts, however, were much more highly correlated (0.73) than found in previous research with older students, thus suggesting that very young children do not make the clear differentiation between these areas found in responses by older children. This research represents an important breakthrough in assessing self-concepts with very young children.

Does self-concept become increasingly multi-dimensional with age? In their original model, Shavelson *et al.* (1976) hypothesised that the multidimensionality of self-concept would increase with age. Although this hypothesis has very important implications for developmental studies of the formation of self-concept, Shavelson *et al.* provided no clear guidance about how to operationalise and test this hypothesis. Marsh and Ayotte (2003) critically evaluated theory and methodology underlying previous tests of this developmental proposal and introduced a new **differential distinctiveness hypothesis**. A new French translation of the SDQ-I was completed by young French-Canadian students in Grades 2–6. Strong psychometric properties, a well defined multidimensional structure, factorial invariance over age, small stereotypic gender differences, largely linear declines in mean levels of self-concept with age, and modest differentiation between academic competence and affect replicated and extended previous research. We developed and provided strong support for a new differential distinctiveness hypothesis. The results showed that with increasing age and cognitive development there are counter-balancing processes of integration and differentiation – increasing integration of closely linked areas of self-concept as well as increasing differentiation of disparate areas of self-concept. Hence, this new operationalisation of the differential distinctiveness hypothesis and the associated results provided a more defensible test and stronger support for this developmental proposal about the increasingly multi-faceted structure of self-concept.

Gender differences in multiple dimensions of self-concept, masculinity and femininity

The richness of gender differences in self-concept cannot be understood from a unidimensional perspective. Although gender differences in self-esteem are very small (Wylie, 1979), small differences favouring boys grow larger through high school and then decline in adulthood (Kling, Hyde *et al.*, 1999). However, these small gender differences in self-esteem mask larger, counterbalancing gender-stereotypic differences in specific components of self-concept (e.g. boys have high math self-concepts, girls have higher verbal self-concept) and this pattern of gender differences is reasonably consistent from early childhood to adulthood (e.g. Crain, 1996; Eccles, Wigfield *et al.*, 1993; Marsh, 1989; 1993a; 1993b).

The research on gender differences in multiple dimensions of self-concept is also relevant to the study of masculinity, femininity and androgyny. Central postulates in androgyny research (e.g. Marsh & Myers, 1986; Marsh & Byrne, 1991) are that masculinity and femininity both contribute to self-concept, but most research has shown that femininity is not related to self-esteem after controlling for the effects of masculinity – leading to what has been referred to as the masculinity model of androgyny. Marsh and Byrne, however, demonstrated that this apparent lack of support for femininity was due in part to an over-reliance on a unidimensional perspective of self-concept, and global self-esteem measures that emphasise stereotypically masculine characteristics such as self-confidence, assertiveness, and a sense of agency. When measures of masculinity and femininity were related to multidimensional self-concept measures, there was support for a logical, *a priori* pattern of relations leading to the development of the differentiated additive androgyny model. Consistently with this model, the relative contributions of masculinity and femininity varied substantially for different areas of self-concept and femininity contributed more positively than masculinity for self-concept domains that were more stereotypically feminine. Marsh and Byrne found that support for the model was consistent across responses by males and females, across self-responses and responses by significant others, and across age groups. This research demonstrates that relations between self-concept, masculinity, and femininity, cannot be adequately understood if the multidimensionality of self-concept is ignored.

Mental Health psychology

On the basis of their review of mental health research, Marsh, Parada and Ayotte (2004) argued that mental health research is still dominated by a unidimensional perspective of self-concept. To demonstrate the importance of a multidimensional perspective, they related responses from the SDQII and the Youth Self-Report, a leading instrument of adolescent mental health problems. They demonstrated that correlations between 11 factors of self-concept and eight mental health problems varied substantially (+0.11 to −0.83; mean $r = -0.35$). Whereas a unidimensional approach would posit homogeneous relations between factors from the two constructs, the observed heterogeneity of these relations clearly identified the need for a multidimensional perspective. Externalising factors (delinquent, aggressive behaviours) were almost unrelated to physical, appearance, and peer self-concepts and only modestly related to global self-esteem, but were substantially related to parents and honesty self-concepts (−0.46 to −0.70); internalising behaviours were substantially related to emotional stability self-concept (−0.71, −0.83) and, to a lesser extent, self-esteem. Relations among 11 self-concept factors could not be explained in terms of one higher-order self-concept factor, relations among the seven mental health problem factors could not be explained in terms of one higher-order mental health factor, and relations between the 11 self-concept and seven mental health factors could not be explained in terms of the correlation between the higher-order self-concept factor and the higher order mental health factor.

In related research, Marsh, Parada *et al.* (2004) evaluated the multidimensional self-concepts of bullies and victims. Despite the generally negative correlations of self-concept with both the bully and victim factors, there was clear support for the need for a multidimensional perspective of self-concept. Although bullying was negatively correlated with most areas of self-concept, the correlations were close to zero for physical ability and physical appearance self-concepts, for same sex and opposite sex self-concept, and for the emotional stability self-concept. Particularly notable, and consistent with the Marsh, Parada *et al.* (2001) study of US students, bullying was somewhat positively correlated with opposite sex self-concept. For victims, the most negative area of self-concept was same sex self-concept– more negative than other areas of self-concept for victims and more negative than experienced by bullies. Victims also fared much worse than bullies in terms of emotional stability self-concept. For bullies, the most negative area of self-concept was honesty/trustworthiness, suggesting that bullies were cognisant of the fact that they are not doing the right thing when they bully other people. More generally, bullies fared worse than victims, with moderate to strong negative correlations between bullying and honesty/trustworthiness, parent, verbal, and school self-concepts. Interestingly, global self-esteem was negatively correlated with both bully and victim factors and the sizes of these negative correlations were very similar. Hence, neither bullies nor victims had particularly good self-concepts, but there were important differences in the multidimensional profiles of self-concept for bullies and victims.

Personality: Relations to 'Big Five' personality constructs

Marsh and Craven (2006) argued that the unidimensional perspective of self-concept still predominates in personality research. Hence, we sought to evaluate the proposal that relations between self-concept, different components of personality (based on responses to the 'Big Five' personality factors), positive and negative components of affect (Positive and Negative Affect Schedule), and Life Satisfaction can be better understood from a multidimensional perspective of self-concept. Confirmatory factor analysis of a German adaptation of the Self Description Questionnaire III demonstrated 17 *a priori*, reasonably independent self-concept factors (M correlation = 0.14; SD = 0.17) that had a highly differentiated pattern of relations with the eight personality factors (i.e. 5 'Big Five' factors, positive affect, negative affect, and life satisfaction). Seven higher-order factors resulted from the 25 first-order (17 self-concept, eight personality) factors; each 'Big Five' personality factor loaded primarily on one higher-order factor along with a distinct set of self-concept factors to which it was most logically related, whereas two of the higher order factors were defined primarily by self-concept factors. Consistently with theory and previous research, math and verbal self-concepts were somewhat negatively related to each other and this extreme domain specificity was reflected in the systematic and substantial relations with academic criteria measures. Non-academic components of self-concept and the eight personality measures (except, perhaps, Openness) were almost unrelated to all academic outcomes. This highly differentiated multivariate pattern of relations argues against the unidimensional perspective of self-concept that is still prevalent in personality research.

Social psychology: Self-other agreement on multiple dimensions of self-concept

Particularly in social psychology and sociology there is a rich theoretical literature, stemming from a symbolic interactionist perspective, on the agreement between self-ratings and inferred self-concept ratings by significant others. More generally, there is considerable interest in how accurately significant others (e.g., peers, employers, family members, teachers) can infer self-concept ratings. In eight MTMM studies, Marsh (1986, 1990b) demonstrated significant agreement between multiple dimensions of self-concepts inferred by primary school teachers and student responses to the SDQI. Marsh and Craven (1991) extended this research in a comparison of the abilities of elementary school teachers, mothers, and fathers to infer multiple self-concepts of preadolescent children. Although there was reasonable self-other agreement overall (Mn $r = 0.41$), responses by mothers and by fathers were slightly more accurate than those by teachers. All three groups were more accurate in their inferences about physical Ability, reading, mathematics and general school self-concepts than for other specific self-concept scales or self-esteem. In two MTMM studies of SDQIII responses by young adults (Marsh & O'Neill, 1984; Marsh & Byrne, 1993), self-other agreement was very high (Mn $r = 0.57$), and four of the scales had self-other correlations over 0.75. Because the average correlation among the 13 SDQIII scales was only 0.09, these results also provided strong support for the discriminant validity of the ratings according both to traditional guidelines and new CFA models of MTMM data. Interestingly, both studies based on children and young adults found that self-other agreement was consistently lower for global self-esteem than for specific components of self-concept. Hence, research on self-other agreement on multiple dimensions of self-concept provides convincing evidence for the convergent and discriminant validity of multidimensional self-concept ratings, and for the construct validity of a multidimensional perspective of self-concept.

Summary of support for multidimensional perspectives in different disciplines

In summary, there is overwhelming support for the multidimensional perspective of self-concept that is the basis of the SDQ instruments and Shavelson *et al.* (1976) model. Despite this growing body of research, much applied research in many disciplines of psychology has relied on a unidimensional perspective of self-concept in which only a single general self-concept scale (like the self-esteem scale on the SDQ instruments or the Rosenberg, 1965, measure) has been considered. Our results strongly supported our claim that such a unidimensional approach cannot adequately reflect the diversity of specific self-concept domains and their relation to different criteria and outcomes. A multidimensional perspective to self-concept can lead to a better understanding of the complexity of self in different contexts, to more accurate predictions of a wide variety of behaviours as well as appropriate outcome measures for diverse interventions, and a deeper understanding of how self-concept relates to other constructs. Over-reliance on a single self-esteem scale and a unidimensional perspective to self-concept is counterproductive in psychological research. On the basis of my research, I recommend that social science researchers abandon unidimensional perspectives of self-concept that are still prevalent is some areas of research, instead embracing a multidimensional perspective that has been productive in many areas of psychological research. In making this recommendation, however, I do not argue that self-esteem should be excluded – indeed, this factor has been retained as part of the SDQ instruments. Rather, I argue that it should be only one of the multidimensional self-concept factors that needs to be considered in order to understand better the relations between self-concept and a diversity of outcome variables in different disciplines of psychological research.

Causal ordering of self-concept and performance

Do changes in academic self-concept lead to changes in subsequent academic achievement? The causal ordering of academic self-concept and academic achievement is, perhaps, the most vexing question in academic self-concept research. This critical question has important theoretical and practical implications, and has been the focus of considerable research.

Byrne (1984) noted that much of the interest in the self-concept/achievement relation stems from the belief that academic self-concept has motivational properties such that changes in academic self-concept will lead to changes in subsequent academic achievement. Calsyn and Kenny (1977) contrasted self-enhancement and skill-development models of the self-concept/achievement relation. According to the self-enhancement model, self-concept is a primary determinant of academic achievement, thus supporting the self-concept enhancement interventions explicit or implicit in many educational programmes. In contrast, the skill development model implies that academic self-concept emerges principally as a consequence of academic achievement so that academic self-concept is enhanced by developing stronger academic skills.

Because self-concept and academic achievement are not readily amenable to experimental manipulations, most research relies on longitudinal panel data in which both self-concept and achievement are measured on at least two occasions (i.e. a two-wave two-variable design) and preferably three or more. Although well-established paradigms to study this problem did not exist prior to the 1980s, more recent developments in the application of structural equation modelling have evolved for the analysis of such longitudinal panel designs. In her classic review of the academic self-concept research, Byrne (1984) proposed three criteria that such studies must satisfy: (a) a statistical relationship must be established; (b) a clearly established time precedence must be established in longitudinal studies; and (c) a causal model must be tested using appropriate statistical techniques such as SEM.

The rationale for the self-enhancement and skill development models is based on an either-or logic; either self-concept causes achievement or achievement causes self-concept. In 1990 I (Marsh, 1990a; also see Marsh, Byrne & Yeung, 1999) argued that this 'winner takes all' (either-or) rationale was inappropriate from both theoretical and statistical perspectives. Theoretically, as clearly articulated in the Shavelson *et al.* (1976) model and most other theoretical accounts of academic self-concept, prior academic accomplishments are important in the formation of subsequent academic self-concept. Thus, it makes no theoretical sense to argue that this linkage does not exist. Hence, the critical issue is whether the linkage from self-concept to subsequent achievement also exists. Furthermore, the size and direction of this critical linkage is more important than whether it is as large as or larger than the corresponding linkage between prior achievement and subsequent self-concept. In part, the rationale for the either-or model was based upon statistical limitations in procedures used to do the analyses. However, with the introduction of structural equation models based on latent constructs, many of these statistical limitations are no longer relevant. Bringing together stronger theoretical and statistical bases for addressing these issues, I (Marsh, 1990a) proposed the reciprocal effects model (REM) of academic self-concept. Figure 3 presents a prototypical REM designed to test the causal ordering of academic self-concept and achievement. The critical issue is whether there are statistically significant paths leading from prior self-concept to subsequent achievement (in support of self-enhancement predictions) and from prior achievement to subsequent self-concept (in support of skill development predictions). Support for the REM requires that both sets of paths are statistically significant, but from the perspective of self-concept theory and practice, the linkages from prior self-concept to subsequent achievement are particularly important.

Classic causal ordering study

In the introduction of the REM, Marsh (1990a) tested the causal ordering of academic self-concept and academic achievement with data from the large, nationally representative US Youth in Transition study (Figure 4). Data was considered from Times 1 (early 10th Grade), 2 (late 11th Grade), 3 (late 12th Grade), and 4 (one year after normal high school graduation). Three latent constructs were considered: academic ability (T1 only) inferred on the basis of four standardised test scores, academic self-concept (T1, T2, and T4) inferred from responses to 2 (T4) or 3 (T1 and T2) self-rating items, and school grades (T1, T2, T3). Analyses were conducted on responses from the 1456 students who had complete data at T1, T2, and T3. The initial a priori model (Figure 4) was based primarily on the temporal ordering of the data collection (i.e. T1 variables precede T2 variables). At T1, there were three constructs: academic ability, school grades, and academic self-concept. Academic ability was posited to precede school grades because students were asked to report their grades from the previous year. Similarly, at T2, school grades preceded academic self-concept. At T3 and at T4, only one construct was considered and no causal ordering was necessary.

Of particular importance are the effects of latent constructs in one wave on latent constructs in subsequent waves (Figure 4). Parameter estimates for the final model

showed that at T2, academic self-concept is influenced by academic ability and T1 academic self-concept, but not T1 grades. At T2 school grades are influenced both by T1 academic self-concept and by T1 school grades. Similarly, school grades at T3 are influenced significantly both by T2 academic self-concept and by T2 grades. Academic self-concept at T4 was influenced significantly by academic self-concept at T2 (there was no T3 academic self-concept measure) but not by T3 school grades. Particularly since the results were replicated across two different intervals, the findings provide strong support for the effect of prior self-concept on subsequent school grades. The Marsh (1990a) study is important because it was one of the first studies – along with, perhaps, Shavelson and Bolus (1982) – to provide defensible evidence for the effect of prior academic self-concept on subsequent academic achievement and because it was apparently methodologically stronger than previous research.

How well do these results generalise to other countries and cultures?

Recent research demonstrated that this support for the REM of academic self-concept and achievement generalised to different cultural/national settings in a large nationally representative sample of Hong Kong students (Marsh, Hau & Kong, 2002) and large samples of East and West German students at the time of the fall of the Berlin Wall (Marsh & Köller, 2003; Marsh, Köller & Baumert, 2001). Support for the generalisability also comes from research based on French-speaking Canadian primary students (Guay, Marsh & Boivin, 2003) and the German high school students (Marsh, Trautwein *et al.*, 2005) described earlier. Hence, there is strong cross-national and cross-cultural support for the REM.

Challenges to support for the REM

Presently there is a 'positive psychology' revolution sweeping psychology, one that emphasises a positive psychology that focuses on

Figure 3: Prototype causal–ordering model for testing self-enhancement, skill–development, and reciprocal–effects models.

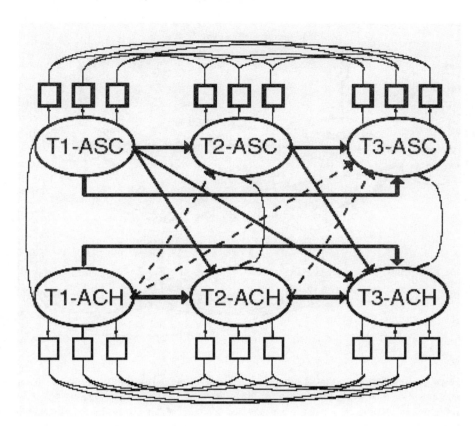

In this full-forward, multiwave, multivariable model, multiple indicators of academic self-concept (ASC) and achievement (ACH) are collected in three successive waves (T1, T2, and T3). Each latent construct (represented by ovals) has paths leading to all latent constructs in subsequent waves. Within each wave, academic self-concept and achievement are assumed to be correlated; in the first wave, this correlation is a covariance between two latent constructs, and in subsequent waves, it is a covariance between residual factors. Curved lines at the top and bottom of the figure reflect correlated uniquenesses between responses to the same measured variable (represented by boxes) collected on different occasions. Paths connecting the same variable on multiple occasions reflect stability (the solid gray paths), but these coefficients typically differ from the corresponding test-retest correlations (which do not include the effects of other variables). Dashed lines reflect effects of prior achievement on subsequent self-concept, whereas solid black lines reflect the effects of prior self-concept on subsequent achievement.

Figure 4: Structural equation model of results from a longitudinal–panel–design study relating academic self-concept on multiple occasions (T1, T2, T3, and T4).

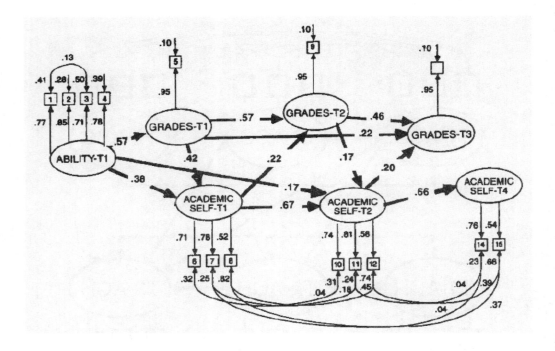

The model shows the standardized effects of academic self-concept on subsequent school grades and academic self-concept. The boxes represent the latent constructs (the ovals). Straight lines connecting the latent constructs, represent coefficients. Nonsignificant paths are excluded for purposes of clarity. The curved lines represent correlated residuals. Of particular relevance are paths (highlighted) leading from prior academic self-concept (ASC) to future grades and those leading from prior grades to future academic self-concept. Adapted with permission from Marsh (1990a, p.650).

how healthy, normal and exceptional individuals can get the most from life. Positive self-beliefs are at the heart of this revolution and this contention is supported by the REM of self-concept and achievement. However, Baumeister, Campbell *et al.* (2003; also see Baumeister, Campbell *et al.*, 2005) have challenged this optimistic perspective in a highly influential review commissioned for *Psychological Science in the Public Interest*, posing the question: 'Does high self-esteem cause better performance, interpersonal success, happiness, or healthier lifestyles?' Drawing a pessimistic conclusion to this question, Baumeister *et al.* (2003) concluded that 'self-esteem *per se* is not the social panacea that many people hoped it was' (p.38), a point reiterated by Baumeister *et al.* (2005) who concluded 'that efforts to boost people's self-esteem are of little value in fostering academic achievement or preventing undesirable behaviour' (p.84).

However, in their influential reviews of the role of self-esteem in educational settings, Baumeister *et al.* (2003, 2005) took an implicitly unidimensional perspective of self-concept, concluding that self-esteem – the global component of self-concept – has no effect on subsequent academic performance. Marsh and Craven (2006) critiqued this review from their multidimensional perspective. In their review they reported clear support for their REM, which posits that academic self-concept and achievement are each a cause and an effect of the other. Baumeister *et al.* had focused primarily on older studies that did not incorporate current statistical methodology and conceptual advances in self-concept theory; Marsh and Craven emphasised studies based on latent variables, structural equation models, and a multidimensional perspective of self-concept. Strangely, none of this more recent research was even considered in Baumeister *et al.* Consequently, the juxtaposition of the reviews by Baumeister *et al.* and by Marsh and Craven, demonstrate the inadequacy of a unidimensional perspective of self-concept, which has already been put into question by more recent research.

It is important to acknowledge that there were important areas of agreement between Baumeister *et al.* (2003) and Marsh and Craven (1997, 2006) on appropriate methodology. In particular, both agreed that correlations based on a single wave of data cannot be used to infer causation, and on the need for longitudinal panel designs (as in the REM) in which achievement and self-beliefs are each measured on at least two different occasions. Noting the strength of longitudinal panel designs, Baumeister *et al.* added the caveat that: 'Insisting that self-esteem [at Time 1] must predict achievement at Time 2 after controlling for achievement at Time 1 could obscure some actual causal relationships, so it should be regarded as a highly conservative way of testing the hypothesis ... one may be throwing a very large baby out with the statistical bathwater' (p.9). Marsh and Craven (1997, 2006) also argued that longitudinal panel designs were the strongest approach to testing the causal ordering of academic self-concept and achievement. However, there were key areas of disagreement between the two sets of reviews in terms of:

a. *Use of current research:* Research into relations between self-beliefs and achievement reviewed by Baumeister *et al.* was all based on publications from 1960 to 1990, whereas research reviewed by Marsh and Craven was conducted almost entirely since 1990, and typically since 2000;

b. *Research methodology:* Research reviewed by Baumeister *et al.* was based largely on multiple regression, which was typical of research of the pre-1990 era, whereas Marsh and Craven (1997, 2006) focused on studies that used structural equation models (SEM) based on multiple indicators;

c. *Unidimensional vs. Multidimensional perspective:* Baumeister *et al.* (2003) focused on an implicit unidimensional perspective of self-concept through their sole reliance on self-esteem – the global component of multidimensional, hierarchical models of self-concept (see Shavelson *et al.*, 1976; Marsh, 1993a). Marsh and Craven (1997, 2006) took an explicitly multidimensional perspective based on multiple, relatively distinct components of self-concept in which they argued that:

if the role of academic self-concept research is to better understand the complexity of self in different contexts, to predict a wide variety of academic behaviours, to provide outcome measures for diverse interventions, and to relate self-concept to other academic constructs, then specific academic domains of self-concept are more useful than global self-esteem. Particularly in educational settings, the clear separation of academic from non-academic self-concept and global self-esteem is very important (Marsh & Craven, 2006, pp.141).

Particularly in educational psychological research, research reviewed earlier (also see Marsh & Craven, 2006) demonstrates that diverse academic outcomes are systematically related to academic self-concept but nearly unrelated (or even negatively related) to global self-esteem and other non-academic components of self-concept. Hence, it is not surprising that prior self-esteem does not have much effect on subsequent academic achievement. In relation to the Baumeister *et al.* (2003, 2005) reviews, the most important counter-argument is the consistent support for REM predictions based on longitudinal panel studies, showing that academic self-concept and achievement are mutually reinforcing constructs, each having an impact on the other.

A critical limitation in reviews by both Baumeister *et al.* (2003; Baumeister *et al.*, 2005) and by Marsh (1993a; Marsh & Craven, 1997, 2006) was the failure to consider studies that included both self-concept and self-esteem. Indeed, even though these reviews addressed basically the same questions about the effects of self-

beliefs on subsequent academic performance, there was almost no overlap in the set of studies that they drew upon to support their apparently contradictory conclusions. However, recent meta-analytic research by Valentine and colleagues (Valentine & DuBois, 2005; Valentine, DuBois & Cooper, 2004) addresses this problem. Based on their comprehensive meta-analysis of all available research, they found consistent support for reciprocal effects between academic self-beliefs and achievement, but little or no reciprocal effect between achievement and self-esteem (also see Trautwein, Lüdtke *et al.*, 2006).

Although reviews by Baumeister *et al.* (2003, 2005) and reviews by Marsh and colleagues yielded apparently contradictory conclusions about the effects of self-beliefs, Marsh and Craven (2006) argued that the findings were not inconsistent. Rather, we concluded that the clear support for effects associated with academic self-concept and the clear lack of effect associated with self-esteem entirely 'reinforces the importance of considering academic self-concept measures in causal-ordering studies of school performance and the need to account for the multidimensionality of the self-concept construct' (Marsh & Craven, 2006, p.150). The apparent disagreement was mostly a function of how the critical questions were asked and what evidence was considered in support of conflicting positions. I agree with the Baumeister *et al.* conclusion that self-esteem has little effect on academic self-concept. However, this unidimensional perspective is entirely consistent and easily incorporated into my multidimensional perspective. The finding that academic self-concept does affect subsequent achievement whereas self-esteem does not provides strong support for the multidimensional perspective, and the REM. Importantly, the apparent controversy is easily resolved by placing it within an appropriate theoretical and statistical perspective.

New directions in tests of the reciprocal effects model

With the hindsight of 15 years' experience, Marsh *et al.* (1999) offered commentary on potential problems and how they can be avoided in future REM research; we demonstrated new, more defensible models of these data, emphasised more generally the role of researcher as substantive data detective and updated Byrne's (1984) standards of an 'ideal' study and directions for future research. Importantly, we also noted important areas in which further research was needed. Here I summarise some subsequent research in response to needs identified by Marsh *et al.*

Does the nature of causal effects vary with age?

I began this section by arguing that the critical question in self-concept research is whether or not there exists a causal link from prior academic self-concept to subsequent achievement. Although there is increasing evidence in support of this effect for older students in middle and high schools, there is a very limited body of strong research and no consistent pattern of results for young students in the early primary school years. This is indeed unfortunate as many researchers and practitioners alike argue that this is a critical time for young children to develop positive self-concepts of themselves as students (e.g. Chapman & Tunmer, 1997; Marsh & Craven, 1997).

Consistently with this concern, Marsh *et al.* (1999) argued that the REM has not been examined fully from a developmental perspective, especially with younger children. Wigfield and Karpathian (1991, p.255) argued that: 'Once ability perceptions are more firmly established the relation likely becomes reciprocal: Students with high perceptions of ability would approach new tasks with confidence, and success on those tasks is likely to bolster their confidence in their ability.' Skaalvik and Hagtvet (1990) found support for a reciprocal effects model for older students (sixth and seven grades) but a skill-development model for younger students (third and fourth grades; see also Muijs, 1997 for similar results). Whereas Skaalvik (1997) also reported support for a skill-development model during elementary school years and reciprocal influences during the high school years, Skaalvik and Valas (1999) did not provide support for this developmental perspective. However, in their review, Marsh *et al.* (1999) argued that that there was insufficient research to determine how well the REM generalises over age, a conclusion echoed by Valentine *et al.* (Valentine & Dubois, 2005; Valentine *et al.*, 2004) in their comprehensive meta-analysis of REM studies.

In order to test the developmental pattern in the causal ordering of these constructs, Marsh *et al.* (1999) recommended the use of multicohort-multioccasion designs (e.g. Marsh *et al.*, 1998) that combined the advantages of cross-sectional (multiple age cohorts) and longitudinal (multiple occasions) research within the same study. Guay *et al.* (2003) pursued this proposal to evaluate developmental hypotheses about the causal ordering of academic self-concept and academic achievement among elementary school children through the use of a multicohort-multioccasion design. (i.e. three age cohorts, each with three measurement waves) for responses by young children in Grades 2, 3, and 4.

The structural equation model for the total sample supported a reciprocal effects model for the first two waves of data (paths leading from prior self-concept to subsequent achievement and from prior achievement to subsequent self-concept) and a self-enhancement effect (paths leading from prior self-concept to subsequent achievement) between the second and the third waves. This pattern was replicated in tests of the invariance of the structural equation model across the three age cohorts (see Figure 5). Based on the preadolescent age groups considered in their study, there was strong support for the generalisability of the reciprocal effects model over age, even for young children.

In contrast to previous research, we (Guay *et al.*, 2003) offer a methodologically strong study that provides clear support for the link between prior academic self-concept and subsequent achievement for young students. Importantly, this result generalised across comparisons based on different age cohorts of young students and different waves within each cohort. Because the Guay *et al.* study is, perhaps, the methodologically strongest study of the causal ordering of academic self-concept differences for young children, it provided important new support for the reciprocal effects model. In particular, it substantially extended our earlier conclusion about the generalisability of the REM. In summary, the results of the Guay *et al.* study provide strong support for the generality over preadolescent ages of this important link between prior self-concept and subsequent achievement.

It is important to emphasise that the present results have important practical implications. The fact that the REM was supported for very young children (i.e. Grade 2) provided support for early interventions based on academic self-concept and achievement, and not only on achievement, as the results of a number of previous studies had suggested (e.g. Chapman & Tunmer, 1997; Helmke & van Haken, 1995; Skaalvik, 1997; Skaalvik & Hagtvet, 1990; Skaalvik & Valas; 1999). Specifically, the Guay *et al.* (2003) results suggest that with young children, teachers should strive to improve simultaneously both academic self-concept and achievement in order to produce positive changes in both these constructs.

How does academic interest fit into the reciprocal effects model?

Because there now exists good support for the reciprocal effects model, there is also a need to pursue further research into the psychological processes that mediate the positive effects of prior academic self-concept on subsequent academic achievement. Implicit in my discussion is the largely untested assumption that the effect of prior self-concept on subsequent achievement is mediated by student characteristics such as increased conscientious effort, persistence in the face of difficulties, enhanced intrinsic motivation, academic choice, and coursework selection (see Marsh *et al.*, 1999). Thus, for example, Marsh and Yeung (1997a, 1997b) found that coursework selection partially mediated the effects of prior academic self-concept in a specific school subject on subsequent achievement in the same subject (e.g. high math self-concept led to taking more advanced math courses, which led to higher levels of math achievement). Clearly, there is a need for more research exploring the psychological processes that mediate the effects of prior academic self-concept on subsequent achievement. Pursuing this important, unresolved issue, Marsh, Trautwein *et al.* (2005) suggested that academic interest might serve this role.

Although academic interest measures and related constructs such as intrinsic motivation are frequently discussed as predictors of achievement and correlates of academic self-concept, these variables had not been integrated into the REMs In collaboration with colleagues from the Max Planck Institute in Berlin, we (Marsh, Trautwein *et al.*, 2005) tested structural equation models of longitudinal data based on two large, nationally representative samples of German high school students. We expanded the typical causal ordering model to include academic interest and two different measures of achievement (grades and achievement test scores) as well as academic self-concept (see Figure 6). The results of both studies were

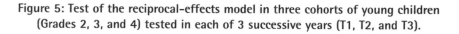

Figure 5: Test of the reciprocal-effects model in three cohorts of young children (Grades 2, 3, and 4) tested in each of 3 successive years (T1, T2, and T3).

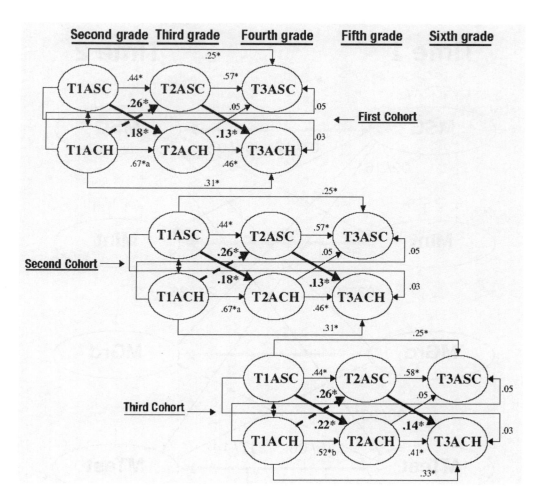

For emphasis, statistically significant paths that are critical for tests of the reciprocal-effects model are presented in bold (dashed lines from prior achievement to subsequent self-concept, solid gray lines from prior self-concept to subsequent achievement). Letters are used to indicate whether the path connecting Time 1 academic achievement with Time 2 academic achievement was invariant (i.e., same letter) or not invariant (i.e. different letter) across the three cohorts. Asterisks indicate significant parameter estimates ($p < 0.05$). ASC = academic self-concept; ACH = academic achievement. Reprinted with permission from Guay, Marsh and Boivin (2003, p.132).

Figure 6: Structural equation model relating math latent constructs at Time 1
to the same constructs at Time 2.

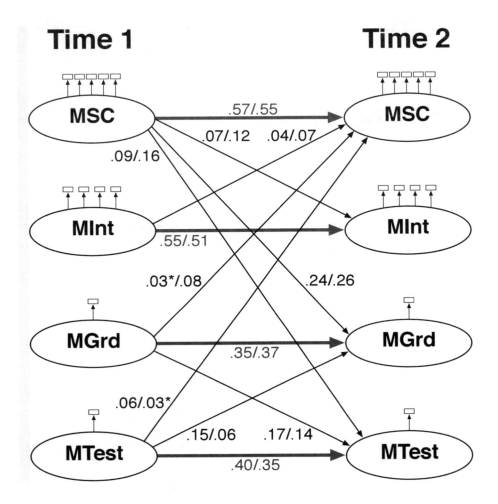

Horizontal paths representing stability between matching T1 and T2 constructs are printed in gray. Results from two separate studies are presented (the two coefficients in each box). Only statistically significant paths are presented (except in the case of a path that was significant in only one of the two studies; in this case, the asterisk indicates the nonsignificant path). SC = self-concept, Int = interest, Grd = grade (school-based performance), Test = achievement (standardised test score). Reprinted with permission from Marsh *et al.* (2005, p.405).

very consistent (see Figure 6). In support of previous research, we found clear support for the REM based on academic self-concept and achievement, demonstrating that the effect of prior math self-concept was substantial for subsequent math school performance as well as for math test scores. Extending previous results, prior self-concept also significantly influenced subsequent measures of academic interest beyond the effects of earlier measures of school performance, achievement test scores, and academic interest. In contrast to these consistent effects of prior academic self-concept, prior academic interest had only a small effect on subsequent academic self-concept and little or no effect on either school performance or test scores. Whereas the results provided some support for reciprocal effects of academic interest and self-concept on each other, the strength of these reciprocal relations was not particularly strong. This pattern of results also suggested that the reciprocal effects of academic self-concept and achievement were mediated by academic interest only to a small degree. More strongly than previous structural equation modelling research, the results of this study demonstrate the positive effects of academic self-concept on academic interest as well as achievement based both on standardised test scores and school-based performance measures.

Does the reciprocal effects model apply to non-academic settings such as elite athletics and social relation problems?

Our academic self-concept research demonstrates that self-concept is an important outcome variable and also plays a central role in mediating the effects of other desirable outcomes. Although the main focus of our research has been in educational psychology settings, important substantive and methodological lessons from this research are also relevant to applications of self-concept to other, related disciplines.

Gymnastics self-concept and achievement in physical education classes. We (Marsh, Chanal et al., 2006) pursued tests of the reciprocal effects, self-enhancement, and skill development models in relation to physical self-concept and performance skills in physical education classes. More specifically, we evaluated predictions about the effects of T1 gymnastics self-concept and T1 gymnastics performance skills collected at the start of a gymnastics training programme on T2 gymnastics self-concept and T2 gymnastics performance skills collected at the end of a 10-week programme. Performance was based on videotapes of each student's performance on a standardised gymnastics performance test that was evaluated by three independent expert judges. Consistent with *a priori* predictions in support of the REM, the effect of T1 gymnastics self-concept on T2 gymnastics performance (0.20) and the effect of T1 gymnastics performance on T2 gymnastics self-concept (0.14) were both highly significant. Consistently with the REM, gymnastics self-concept and gymnastics performance were both determinants and consequences of each other.

Physical self-concept, health-related physical activity and physical education. We (Marsh, Papaioannou & Theodorakis, 2006) adapted the REM in a study of the causal ordering of physical self-concept and exercise behaviour. Based on a large sample of Greek physical education students (N = 2786 students) collected early (T1) and late (T2) in the school year, analyses supported REM predictions (Figure 7): prior (T1) physical self-concept and exercise behaviour each influenced both subsequent (T2) physical self-concept and exercise behaviour. Consistently with REM predictions, both the effect of T1 physical self-concept on T2 exercise behaviour (0.17) and the effect of T1 exercise behaviour on T2 physical self-concept paths (0.10) were highly significant. In subsequent analyses key constructs from the theory of planned behaviour (behavioural intentions, perceived behavioural control, exercise attitudes) also contributed to the prediction of subsequent exercise behaviour. However, the effect of physical self-concept was significant even after controlling for these additional variables, suggesting that self-concept should be used to supplement the theory of planned behaviour. In further discussion, we contrasted how structural equation modelling had been used in typical tests of the REM in self-concept research and models based on the theory of planned behaviour – and how each area of research could profit from the methodological approaches of the other.

Generalisability to Championship Performances in Elite Swimming. Marsh and Perry (2005) tested REM predictions based on a large sample of many of the best swimmers in the world competing at the Pan Pacific Swimming Championships in Australia and the World Short Course Championships in Greece. Top swimmers from 30 countries completed the 29-item Elite Swimmer SDQ (ESSDQ) instrument on the first day for each of these championships – prior to actually competing in any events. Also available for all participants were previous personal best performances (PPBs in each of their events and, subsequently, actual championship performance. The strongest predictor of championship performance was PPB (path coefficient = 0.87, Figure 8). We evaluated first-order and higher-order factor models in which the six ESSDQ factors are posited to reflect one (global) elite athlete higher-order factor (Figure 8). The goodness of fit and interpretation of both the first-order and higher-order models were similar, as were their interpretations. Whereas the path from the PPB (0.87) to championship perform-ance was substantial, elite athlete self-concept contributed significantly to predicting cham-pionship performance (0.12) beyond what could be explained by PBB. These results are consistent with both the design of the ESSDQ and the global nature of the outcome vari-able (championship performance) – as well as the reciprocal effects model.

Because most swimmers competed in at least two events, we compared results based on their first two events. The effect of global swimmer self-concept on championship performance was highly significant and approximately the same for both events (0.13 and 0.12, respectively). Adapting tradi-tional tests of factorial invariance to this 'within-swimmer' design, we evaluated the replicability of the results across the two events by systematically evaluating the invari-ance of matching pairs of parameters. There was good support for the invariance of all parameter estimates. In summary, elite athlete self-concepts have an effect on the subsequent championship performances of elite swimmers beyond that which can be explained in terms of PPBs and these results were replicated across different events swum by each swimmer.

Summary: Causal ordering of self-concept and performance

The results of causal modelling studies provide a clear affirmative answer to the question 'Do changes in academic self-concept lead to changes in subsequent academic achievement?' This research is critically important in that it has established that increases in academic self-concept lead to increases in subsequent academic achievement and other desirable educa-tional outcomes. Hence, not only is self-concept an important outcome variable in itself, it also plays a central role in mediating the effects of other desirable educational outcomes. These findings have significant implications for international educational policy and practice.

It is important to emphasise that the direction of causality between academic self-concept and achievement has very impor-tant practical implications for educators. If the direction of causality were from academic self-concept to achievement (the self-enhancement model), then teachers might be justified in placing more effort into enhancing students' self-concepts rather than fostering achievement. On the other

Figure 7: Summary of structural equation models predicting future physical self-concept and exercises behaviour from prior physical self-concept and exercise behaviour (A) and the same model with the inclusion of variables from the theory of planned behaviour (for further information, see Marsh, Trautwein *et al.*, 2006).

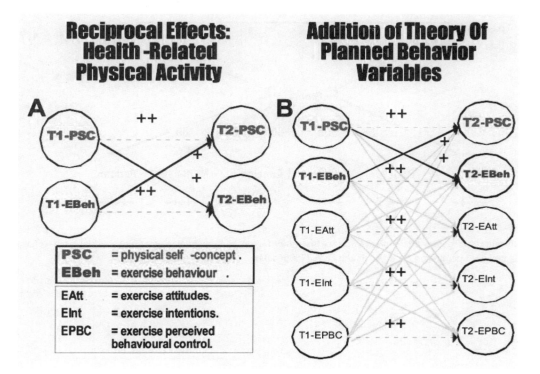

Figure 8: Summary of structural equation models predicting subsequent championship performance ('Champion Perform') on the basis of prior personal best and self-concept responses.

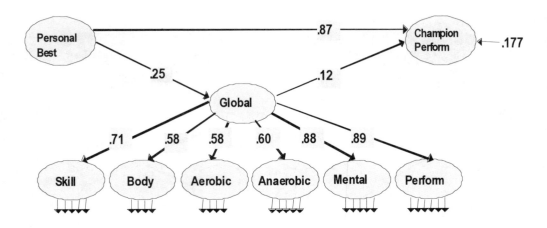

Self-concept responses are represented as six first-order factors and one higher-order global athletic self-concept. Adapted with permission from Marsh and Perry (2005, p.84).

hand, if the direction of causality were from achievement to self-concept (the skill development model), then teachers should focus primarily on improving academic skills as the best way to improve self-concept. In contrast to both these apparently overly simplistic (either-or) models, the reciprocal effects model implies that academic self-concept and academic achievement are reciprocally related and mutually reinforcing. Improved academic self-concepts will lead to better achievement AND improved achievement will lead to better academic self-concepts. For example, if teachers enhance students' academic self-concepts without improving achievement, then the gains in self-concept are likely to be short-lived. However, if teachers improve students' academic achievement without also fostering students' self-beliefs in their academic capabilities, then the achievement gains are also unlikely to be long lasting. If teachers focus on either one of these constructs to the exclusion of the other, then both are likely to suffer. Hence, according to the reciprocal effects model, teachers should strive to improve simultaneously both academic self-concept and achievement.

Frame of reference models of self-concept

Self-concept theory emphasises that perceptions of the self cannot be adequately understood if the role of frames of reference is ignored. The same objective characteristics and accomplishments can lead to disparate self-concepts depending on the frames of reference or standards of comparison that individuals use to evaluate themselves, and these self-beliefs have important implications for future choices, performance, and behaviours. Psychologists from at least the time of William James (1890) have recognised that objective accomplishments are evaluated in relation to frames of reference. Here I describe research evaluating the Internal/External Frame of Reference (I/E) model and the big-fish-little-pond effect (BFLPE).

Why are math and verbal self-concepts so distinct? The Internal/External Frame of Reference (I/E) Model

The I/E model was developed to explain why math and verbal self-concepts are so distinct. This finding has important theoretical, substantive, and practical implications. Theroretically, it was contrary to predictions based on the original Shavelson model of self-concept (Figure 1) and led to the Marsh/Shavelson revision of the model (Figure 2). Substantively, it means that even academic self-concept is highly domain specific. Practically, it means that educational psychologists should be careful to measure academic self-concept at a level of specificity that is appropriate to the aims of their research and the goals of their interventions.

In educational settings, even after students obtain information from various sources about their levels of academic ability and accomplishments, these impressions must be compared to some standard or frame of reference. To the extent that individuals have different frames of reference, the same objective indicators will lead to different academic self-concepts. There is a long history of social comparison research in which it is posited that students evaluate their own performance in relation to external criteria or the performances of other students. This does not explain, however, why academic self-concepts are so content-specific.

Theoretical rationale

The I/E model (for further discussion, see Marsh, 1986, 1990a, 1993a; Marsh et al., 1988; Marsh & Yeung, 2001) was initially developed to explain why math and verbal self-concepts are almost uncorrelated even though corresponding areas of academic achievement are substantially correlated (typically 0.5 to 0.8, depending on how achievement is measured). Individuals who are good in one area tend to be good in the other, but people think of themselves as 'math' persons or 'verbal' persons. According to the I/E model, academic self-concept in a particular school subject is formed in relation to two comparison processes or frames of reference. The first is the typical *external* (normative) reference in which students compare their self-perceived performances in a particular school subject with the perceived performances of other students in the same school subject and other external standards of actual achievement levels. If they perceive themselves to be able in relation to other students and to objective indicators of achievement, then they should have a high academic self-concept in that school subject.

The second is an *internal* (ipsative-like) reference in which students compare their own performance in one particular school subject with their own performances in other school subjects. (Note: ipsative scores sum to a constant so that an increase in any one means that the average of the others much decrease.) If, for example, mathematics is their best school subject, then they should have a positive math self-concept that is higher than their verbal self-concept.

To clarify how these two processes operate, consider a student who accurately perceives him or herself to be below average in both verbal and math skills (an external comparison), but who is better at mathematics than verbal and other school subjects (an internal comparison). The student's math skills are below average relative to other students and objective indicators of math achievement (the external comparison), and this should lead to a below-average math self-concept. However, this student's math skills are above average relative to his or her other school subjects (an internal comparison) and this should lead to an above-average math self-concept. Depending upon how these two processes are weighted and their relative magnitude in the formation of self-concept, this student may have an average or even above-average math self-concept even though he or she has below-average math skills. The I/E model also predicts that this student would have a better math self-concept than another student who did equally poorly at mathematics but who did better in all other school subjects (i.e. math was his or her worst subject). Similarly, a student who is very bright in all school subjects may have an average or even below-average math self-concept if the student perceived mathematics to be his or her worst subject.

The external comparison process should result in substantial positive correlations between math and verbal self-concepts because math and verbal achievements are substantially positively correlated. However, the ipsative, internal comparison process should result in a negative correlation between math and verbal self-concepts because the average correlation among ipsative scores is necessarily negative (i.e. an increase in any one score must result in a counterbalancing decrease in average of the remaining scores if they are ipsative). Both these processes, however, affect self-concept responses. Hence, the joint operation of these processes, depending on the relative weight given to internal and external comparisons, is consistent with the near-zero correlation between math and verbal self-concepts that led to the development of the I/E model. It is, however, important to emphasise that support for the I/E model does not require the correlation between math and verbal self-concepts to be zero, but only that it be substantially less than the typically substantial positive correlation between math and verbal achievement.

Stronger tests of the I/E model are possible when math and verbal achievements are related to math and verbal self-concepts (see Figure 9). The external comparison process predicts that good math skills lead to higher math self-concepts and that good verbal skills lead to higher verbal self-concepts. According to the internal comparison process, however, good math skills should lead to a lower verbal self-concept (once the positive effects of good verbal skills are controlled). The better I am at mathematics, the poorer I perceive myself to be at verbal subjects (relative to my good math skills). Similarly, better verbal skills should lead to a lower math self-concept (once the positive effects of good math skills are controlled). In models used to test this prediction (Figure 9), the horizontal paths leading from math achievement to math self-concept and from verbal achievement to verbal self-concept (horizontal paths in Figure 9) are predicted to be substantially positive (indicated by '++' in Figure 9). However, the cross paths leading from math achievement to verbal self-concept and from verbal achievement to math self-concept are predicted to be negative.

Research evidence

It is not surprising, of course, that good verbal skills are associated with good verbal self-concepts and that good math skills are associated with good math self-concepts (the positive 'horizontal' paths in Figure 9). More surprising – even paradoxical prior to the development of the I/E model – are the negative paths from verbal achievement to math self-concept and from math achieve-

Figure 9: Predicted relations between achievement and self-concept in the math and verbal domains.

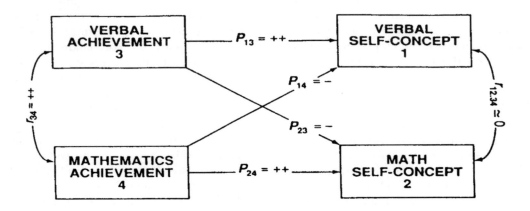

Predictions are based on the internal/external frame-of-reference model. The horizontal paths from achievement to self-concept within content areas are predicted to be substantial and positive (++), whereas the cross paths from achievement in one content area to self-concept in the other content area are predicted to be smaller and negative (–).

ment to verbal self-concept (the negative cross paths in Figure 9). Thus, according to this model, being more mathematically able detracts from verbal self-concept whereas being more verbally able detracts from math self-concept) In a review of 13 studies that considered students of different ages and different academic achievement indicators, Marsh (1986) reported that:

- correlations between indicators of verbal and math achievement were substantial (0.42 to 0.94);
- correlations between measures of verbal and math self-concepts were much smaller (−0.10 to +0.19);
- path coefficients from verbal achievement to verbal self-concept, and from math achievement to math self-concept were all significantly *positive*;
- path coefficients from math achievement to verbal self-concept, and from verbal achievement to math self-concept, were significantly *negative*.

This pattern of results was subsequently replicated for responses to each of three different self-concept instruments by Canadian high school students (Marsh *et al.*, 1988), for the nationally representative sample of US high school students in the High School and Beyond Study (Marsh, 1989), and for the nationally representative sample of US high school students in the National Longitudinal Study (Marsh, 1994). Although much of this support is based on responses by students from the US, Canada, and Australia where the native language is English, there is also some support for the cross-cultural or cross-nationality generalisability of these results where verbal self-concept is in relation to a native language other than English (e.g. Norwegian: Skaalvik & Rankin, 1995; Chinese: Marsh, Kong & Hau, 2001).

Particularly interesting research in Germany (e.g. Möller & Köller 2001) provided support for the I/E in a true experimental study with randomly assigned students, demonstrating how experimentally manipulated feedback on achievement in

one subject area had an inverse effect on self-concept in a different area. The authors concluded that 'as shown experimentally for the first time, dimensional comparison information can have inverse effects on task-related cognitions in other domains' (p.833). Importantly, they demonstrated simultaneous support for both the internal comparison process (based on experimentally manipulated feedback about the relative performance in two different tasks) and the external comparison process (based on experimentally manipulated feedback about performance relative to other students). This research is important, using a true experimental design with random assignment to groups to support causality in the causal path models that are the basis of the I/E model.

Cross-cultural comparisons

Pursuing the important cross-cultural theme of this research, Marsh and Hau (2004) tested the generality of the I/E model based on a cross-cultural study of nationally representative samples of 15-year-olds from 26 countries (total N = 55,577). The PISA database was collected in response to the need for internationally comparable evidence of student performance and related competencies within a common framework that was internationally agreed upon. Selection of the measures was made on the basis of advice from substantive and statistical expert panels and results from extensive pilot studies. Substantial efforts and resources were devoted to achieving cultural and linguistic breadth in the assessment materials, stringent quality-assurance mechanisms were applied in the translation of materials into different languages, and data were collected under independently supervised test conditions (see OECD PISA website for more details).

In preliminary analyses based on the total group, Marsh and Hau (2004) found good support for the I/E model (Figure 10). As predicted, the two horizontal paths relating math achievement to math self-concept (0.44) and relating reading achievement to verbal self-concept (0.47) were substantial and positive, whereas the two cross paths leading from reading achievement to math self-concept (−0.20) and mathematics achievement to verbal self-concept (−0.26) were negative. Also of relevance is the observation that the (zero-order) correlation between math and verbal achievement factors ($r = 0.78$) was very large, whereas the corresponding correlation between math and verbal self-concept factors ($r = 0.10$) was substantially lower.

Marsh and Hau then conducted multigroup CFAs and SEMs in which they constrained different parameters to be invariant across the 26 groups. Although the imposition of these added invariance constraints resulted in small decrements in fit, even the highly restrictive model of total invariance (i.e., requiring every parameter to be the same in all 26 groups) provided a good fit to the data which differed only slightly from the baseline model with no invariance constraints. When results were considered separately for each of the 26 countries (Table 1), there was remarkably good support for the generalisability of major predictions from the I/E model. Whereas math and verbal achievements were substantially correlated in all 26 countries (M $r = 0.76$), math and verbal self-concepts were nearly uncorrelated in all 26 countries (M $r = 0.06$). Of particular relevance, the cross-paths leading from math achievement to verbal self-concept (M $r = -0.22$) and from verbal achievement to math self-concept (M $r = -0.21$) were significantly negative in almost all of the 26 countries.

Summary and implications of the Internal/External frame of reference (I/E) model

There is a wide ranging basis of support for detailed predictions based on the I/E model from individual studies summarised here (also see Marsh, 1986; Marsh & Craven, 2002), the Marsh and Hau (2004) crossnational study of 26 countries, and a recent meta-analysis of I/E studies (Möller,

Pohlmann *et al.*, 2006). The extreme domain specificity of academic self-concepts that led to the development of the I/E model, and which has so convincingly been demonstrated in I/E studies, provides strong support for a multidimensional perspective that is so fundamental to my research programme. These results demonstrate that even global measures of academic self-concept are not sufficient to afford an understanding of the interplay between self-perceptions in different academic domains that is the basis of the internal comparison process in the I/E model.

The extreme domain specificity of academic self-concepts that led to the development of the I/E model also has practical implications for teachers and parents, and for educational practice. Teachers, in order to understand the academic self-concepts of their students in different content areas, must understand the implications of the I/E model. When teachers were asked to infer the self-concepts of their students (see discussion by Marsh & Craven, 1997), their responses reflected primarily the external comparison process so that teachers' inferences were not nearly so domain-specific as responses by their students; students who were bright in one area tended to be seen as having good academic self-concepts in all areas, whereas students who were not bright in one area were seen as having poor academic self-concept in all areas. Similarly, Dai (2002) reported that inferred self-concept ratings by parents reflected primarily the external comparison process typically emphasised in social comparison research, but not the internal comparison process that is the unique feature of the I/E model. In contrast to inferred self-concept ratings by significant others (teachers and parents), students' academic self-concepts in different domains are extremely differentiated. Hence, understanding the implications of the I/E model will allow significant others to better understand children and to infer children's self-concepts more accurately. Thus, for example, our results demonstrate

Figure 10: Relations between achievement and self-concept in the math and verbal domains (also see Figure 7) from analyses of responses from 15-year-olds from 26 countries.

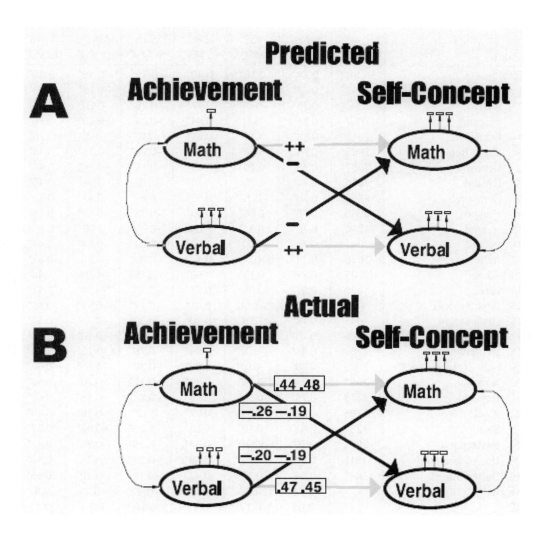

Within each box, the first number comes from the total-group analysis, and the second number comes from a multiple-group analysis in which each country was considered separately, but the results were constrained to be equal across countries. Adapted with permission from Marsh and Hau (2004, p.58).

Table 1: Summary of tests of the Internal/External frame of reference model for each of 26 different countries (see also Figure 9).

Country		N	Factor Corr		Path Coefficients			
			MAch Vach	VSC MSC	From MAch to MSC	From VAch to MSC	From MAch to VSC	From VAch to VSC
Total		55,582	0.78*	0.10*	0.48*	−0.19*	−0.19*	0.45*
1	Australia	2642	0.77*	0.08*	0.41*	−0.16*	−0.19*	0.39*
2	Austria	2380	0.76*	−0.07*	0.47*	−0.25*	−0.26*	0.56*
3	Belgium	1962	0.81*	−0.11*	0.34*	−0.24*	−0.20*	0.26*
4	Brazil	2218	0.69*	0.14*	0.23*	−0.07	−0.08	0.25*
5	Czech Republic	2698	0.74*	0.08*	0.51*	−0.22*	−0.17*	0.48*
6	Denmark	2087	0.78*	0.10*	0.65*	−0.18*	−0.16*	0.48*
7	Finland	2576	0.71*	0.28*	0.70*	−0.06	0.04	0.46*
8	Germany	2502	0.79*	−0.12*	0.62*	−0.45*	−0.41*	0.60*
9	Hungary	2550	0.76*	0.08*	0.43*	−0.15*	−0.17*	0.49*
10	Iceland	1720	0.75*	0.31*	0.68*	−0.09*	0.08	0.40*
11	Ireland	2041	0.79*	−0.11*	0.53*	−0.22*	−0.44*	0.47*
12	Italy	2678	0.73*	−0.06*	0.49*	−0.21*	−0.35*	0.62*
13	Korea	2705	0.77*	0.13*	0.58*	−0.19*	−0.04	0.48*
14	Latvia	1920	0.61*	0.09*	0.37*	−0.20*	−0.14*	0.47*
15	Liechtenstein	153	0.76*	−0.06	0.41*	−0.27*	−0.37*	0.55*
16	Luxembourg	1441	0.74*	0.01	0.40*	−0.30*	−0.27*	0.57*
17	Mexico	2275	0.76*	0.52*	0.14*	−0.03	−0.10*	0.20*
18	Netherlands	1282	0.84*	−0.07*	0.89*	−0.75*	−0.25*	0.34*
19	New Zealand	1809	0.80*	−0.07*	0.80*	−0.38*	−0.53*	0.68*
20	Norway	2050	0.73*	0.14*	0.72*	−0.17*	−0.20*	0.59*
21	Portugal	2378	0.79*	0.06*	0.55*	−0.28*	−0.18*	0.48*
22	Russia	3398	0.68*	0.29*	0.22*	0.12*	−0.16*	0.49*
23	Sweden	2282	0.81*	0.18*	0.58*	−0.20*	−0.08*	0.37*
24	Switzerland	2982	0.76*	−0.20*	0.54*	−0.39*	−0.28*	0.42*
25	United Kingdom	1211	0.82*	−0.12*	0.69*	−0.27*	−0.38*	0.45*
26	United States	1642	0.84*	0.11*	0.42*	−0.15*	−0.20*	0.55*
Mean			0.76	0.06	0.51	−0.22	−0.21	0.47
SD			0.05	0.17	0.18	0.16	0.14	0.12
Median			0.74	0.08	0.52	−0.20	−0.20	0.48
25th %tile			0.76	−0.07	0.41	−0.27	−0.30	0.40
75th %tile			0.79	0.14	0.66	−0.15	−0.13	0.55

Note: All parameter estimates are present in completely standardised form. Factor correlations are based on a confirmatory factor analysis model, whereas path coefficients are based on a structural equation model. The total results based on all 26 countries. MAch = math achievement; VAch = verbal achievement; MSC = math self-concept; VSC = verbal self-concept; corr = correlation. Adapted with permission from Marsh and Hau (2004)

* $p < 0.05$.

that even bright students may have an average or below-average self-concept in their weakest school subject which may seem paradoxical, in relation to their good achievement (good relative to other students, but not to their own performance in other school subjects). Similarly, even poor students may have an average or above average self-concept in their best school subject that may seem paradoxical in relation to their below-average achievement in that subject. Particularly for weaker students, understanding these principles should assist teachers and parents to give positive feedback that is credible to students.

Big-Fish–Little-Pond effect

The historical and theoretical underpinnings of this research (see Marsh, 1974, 1984, 1991, 1993a; Marsh & Parker, 1984) were derived from research in psychophysical judgment (e.g. Helson, 1964; Marsh, 1974; Parducci, 1995), social judgment (e.g. Morse & Gergen, 1970; Sherif & Sherif, 1969; Upshaw, 1969), sociology (Alwin & Otto, 1977; Hyman, 1942; Meyer, 1970), social comparison theory (e.g. Festinger, 1954; Suls, 1977), and the theory of relative deprivation (Davis, 1966; Stouffer *et al.*, 1949).

In my research programme I have translated materials from a variety of different theoretical frameworks into an educational setting. In the theoretical model underlying the BFLPE, Marsh (1984) hypothesised that students compare their own academic ability with the academic abilities of their peers and use this social comparison impression as one basis for forming their own academic self-concept. A negative BFLPE occurs when equally able students have lower academic self-concepts when they compare themselves to more able students, and higher academic self-concepts when they compare themselves with less able students. For example, consider average ability students who attend a high-ability school (i.e. a school where the average ability level of other students is high). Because students' academic skills are below the average of other students in their school, it is predicted that this will lead to academic self-concepts that are below average. Conversely, if these students attended a low ability school, then their abilities would be above average in that school. This would lead to academic self-concepts that are above average. Thus, academic self-concepts depend not only on one's own academic accomplishments but also on the accomplishments of classmates in the school that a student attends. According to this model, academic self-concept will be correlated positively with individual achievement (higher achieving children will have higher

academic self-concepts). However, academic self-concept should be negatively related to school-average achievement (equally able students will have lower academic self-concepts in a school where the average ability is high and higher academic self-concepts in a school where the average ability is low). In the most basic version of this model (Figure 11) it is hypothesised that the effect of individual student ability on individual student academic self-concept is positive, whereas the effect of school or class-average ability is negative.

Empirical support for the BFLPE comes from numerous studies (e.g. Marsh, 1984, 1987, 1994; Marsh & Craven, 1994, 1997; Marsh & Parker, 1984; see review by Marsh & Craven, 2002) based on a variety of different experimental/analytical approaches. In the first small study in this research programme, we (Marsh & Parker, 1984; see Figure 12) sampled sixth grade classes from high and low socioeconomic status SES areas in the same geographical area. The two samples differed substantially in terms of reading achievement and IQ scores. In path models of the relations among achievement, school-average ability and responses to the Self-Description Questionnaire-I (SDQI; Marsh, 1990c), the direct effect of school-average ability on academic self-concept was negative in models that controlled for individual achievement. In contrast, the effects of individual and school-average achievement were not statistically significant for non-academic self-concept. Hence, the results provided an early demonstration of the BFLPE and its specificity to academic components of self-concept.

In an American study based on 88 high schools, I (Marsh, 1987; see Figure 12; also see Bachman & O'Malley, 1986) found that the effects of school-average ability on academic self-concept were negative, whereas the effects of school-average SES on academic self-concept were negligible. He also found that African-American students,

Figure 11: Path Model Predictions based on the big–fish–little–pond effect.

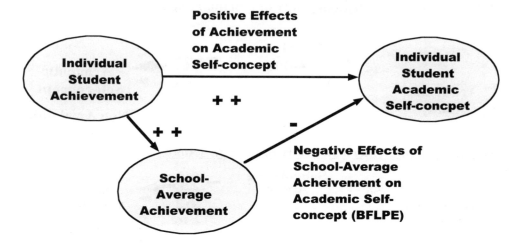

Figure 12: Summary of results based on two early studies of the big-fish-little-pond effect.

Results from an Australian Study of 6 primary schools

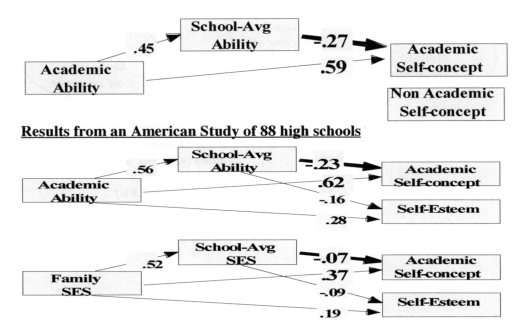

Results from an American Study of 88 high schools

(A) A small Australian study based on six primary schools (see Marsh & Parker, 1984). (B) A large American study based on the Youth in Transition data (Marsh, 1987). Separate analyses were conducted on individual and school-average measures of academic ability and socioeconomic status.

particularly those in segregated schools, did not differ substantially from Caucasian students in terms of academic self-concept even though there were substantial differences in terms of standardised achievement test scores. Whereas this pattern might suggest that the academic self-concept responses were 'culturally biased', this is exactly the pattern predicted to occur in the BFLPE. African Americans had academic ability test scores that were below average, but – particularly in the segregated schools – compared themselves to classmates who also had below-average test scores. Thus, while their academic self-concepts were somewhat below average (due, perhaps to self-perceptions that were independent of the immediate school context), they were not nearly as low as ability tests would suggest.

This study (Marsh, 1987) also clarified the distinction between academic ability and grade-point average (GPA), their respective influences on self-concept, and how this influenced the BFLPE. The 88 schools in the study differed substantially in terms of school-average academic ability, but not of school-average GPA. Schools 'graded on a curve' so that grade distributions (e.g. the percentage of students getting high grades) were similar from one school to the next even though academic ability levels differed substantially. Hence, equally able students have lower GPAs in high-ability schools than in low-ability schools. Marsh demonstrated that this frame of reference effect influencing GPA was separate from, but contributed to, the BFLPE on academic self-concept. In further analysis of this same data, Marsh and Rowe (1996) replicated the finding using a multilevel modelling approach and demonstrated that the BFLPE generalised across all levels of initial ability level, including the very brightest students. More recently, we (Trautwein, Lüdtke *et al.*, in press) found a similar phenomenon in German high schools. Consistently with my 1987 study, we found that the inclusion of school grades substantially increased the percentage of explained variance in academic self-concept beyond what could be explained in terms of standardised test scores and reduced somewhat the BFLPE (the negative effect of school-average achievement). Whereas both studies showed that the BFLPE and the phenomenon of grading on a curve are mutually reinforcing, both studies showed that the BFLPE cannot be explained in terms of grading on a curve.

Sociologists studying school context effects have found that school-average ability and particularly school-average SES are related to educational and occupational aspirations or attainments. In a review of this largely American literature, Alwin and Otto (1977) reported that school-average ability was negatively related to aspirations, whereas school-average SES tended to be positively associated with aspirations. Marsh (1991) also showed that school-average ability was negatively related to academic self-concept as well as a number of other educational outcome variables in a large, nationally representative American sample. In fact, one of the original inspirations for the BFLPE was Davis's (1966) study of career decisions of American college students. Davis sought support for a theoretical explanation of why the academic quality of a college had so little effect on career choice and occupational aspirations. Expanding the educational policy implications of his research, Davis (1966, p.31) concluded:

> Counsellors and parents might well consider the drawbacks as well as the advantages of sending a boy to a 'fine' college, if, when doing so, it is fairly certain that he will end up in the bottom ranks of his graduating class. The aphorism 'It is better to be a big frog in a small pond than a small frog in a big pond' is not perfect advice but it is not trivial.

Such advice may also be relevant for evaluating the likely impact of attending academically selective high schools.

Rogers, Smith and Coleman (1978) ranked a group of children in terms of academic achievement relative to their own classroom and academic achievement across the sample. They found that the within class-room rankings were correlated more highly with self-concept than scores normed in relation to the entire sample.

Schwarzer, Jerusalem and Lange (1983; also see Jerusalem, 1984) examined the self-concepts of West German students who moved from non-selective, heterogeneous primary schools to secondary schools that were streamed on the basis of academic achievement. At the transition point students selected to enter the high ability schools had substantially higher academic self-concepts than those entering the low ability schools. However, by the end of the first year in the new schools no differences in academic self-concepts for the two groups were present. Path analyses indicated that the direct influence of school type on academic self-concept was negative. Thus, the most able students in the low ability schools were less able but had much higher academic self-concepts than the least able children in the high ability schools.

Brookover (1989) examined frame-of-reference effects on academic self-concept from the perspective of the extent to which students in different schools were streamed according to ability. In schools with ability streaming, low-ability students tended to be placed in classes with other low-ability students and high-ability students tended to be placed in classes with other high-ability students. To the extent that students use other students within their class as a frame of reference, low-ability students in streamed classes should have higher academic self-concepts (because they compare themselves primarily to other low-ability students) than low-ability students in unstreamed classes. High-ability students in streamed classes, however, should have lower academic self-concepts (because they compare themselves primarily to other high-ability students) than high-ability students in unstreamed classes. Thus, streaming should tend to increase the academic self-concepts of low-ability students and decrease the academic self-concepts of high-ability

students. Consistently with these predictions, Brookover found that the academic self-concepts were much less variable in schools that streamed their classes.

Zeidner and Schleyer (1999) tested the BFLPE in a large-scale study based on a nationally representative sample ($N = 1020$) of Israeli gifted students participating in either special homogenous classes for the gifted or mixed ability classes. Path analyses indicated that gifted students in mixed ability classes evidenced markedly higher academic self-concepts, lower anxiety and higher school grades than gifted students in specialised classes.

So what if students have lower self-concept in academically selective schools?

The clear, consistent support for the BFLPE is very exciting for self-concept researchers, and important for understanding the formation of academic self-concept and for testing frame of reference models. However, classroom teachers, policy makers and particularly parents might be prompted to ask 'So what?' What are the consequences of attending high-ability schools on other academic outcomes and how are these related to academic self-concept? In order to address these issues, I (Marsh, 1991) considered the influence of school-average ability on a much wider array of outcomes and the role of academic self-concept and educational aspirations formed early in high school as mediators of the effects of school-average ability on subsequent outcomes. The High School and Beyond data were ideal for this purpose because the database is very large (1000 randomly selected high schools and approximately 30 randomly selected students from each school), nationally representative of the US, and contains longitudinal data, consisting of responses by the same high school students when they were sophomores (T1), seniors (T2), and two years after the normal graduation from high school (T3). The major components of the path analysis (see Figure 13) in this

Figure 13: Testing the implications of the big-fish-little-pond effect, the effect of school-average ability (mean ability), on a diverse range of educational outcomes collected in Year 10 (sophomore year of high school, Time 1), Year 12 (senior year of high school, Time 2), and two years after the normal graduation from high school (Time 3).

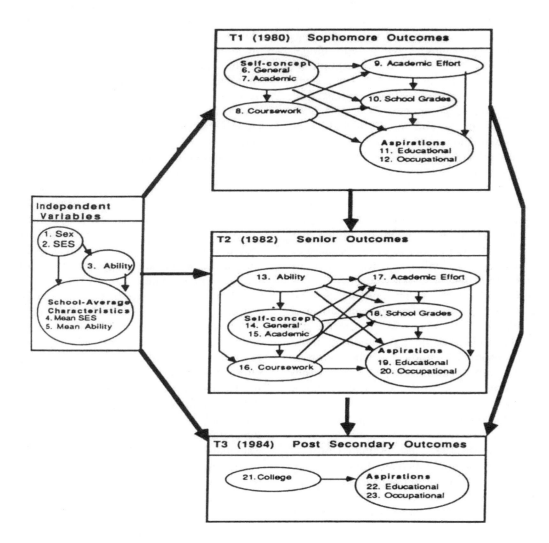

research were: (a) individual-level and school-average measures of academic ability (a battery of standardised tests) and SES; (b) self-concept (academic and general), academic choice behaviour (taking advanced coursework), academic effort (time spent on homework and class preparation), school grades (GPA), educational aspirations, and occupational aspirations measured at T1 and T2, and (c) college attendance, educational aspirations, and occupational aspirations at T3.

Although the path model including all these outcome variables is complicated, the results are easy to summarise. The effects of school-average ability were negative for almost all of the T1, T2, and T3 outcomes; 15 of the 17 relations were significantly negative and two were not statistically significant. Even though it might be argued that most of the important outcome variables in educational research were considered in this study, the effect of school-average ability was not positive for a single outcome. School-average ability most negatively affected academic self-concept as in the BFLPE studies and educational aspirations as in the school-context studies. School-average ability also negatively affected general self-concept, coursework selection, school grades, standardised test scores, occupational aspirations, and subsequent college attendance.

I (Marsh, 1991) also evaluated process variables that might mediate the subsequent negative effects of school-average ability. Controlling T1 academic self-concept and T1 educational aspirations substantially reduced the negative effects of school-average ability at T2 and T3. This supported their proposed role as mediating variables. Even after controlling all T1 outcomes, however, school-average ability negatively affected seven of 11 outcomes at T2 and T3. This demonstrated that school-average ability continued to affect T2 and T3 outcomes negatively beyond its already substantial negative effects at T1. The largest of these negative effects was for T2 academic self-concept. When T2 academic self-concept was also controlled, the remaining school-average ability effects were less negative. This study demonstrated the importance of academic self-concept as both a proximal outcome and a mediating variable that facilitated the attainment of more distal outcomes.

In summary, equally able students attending higher-ability high schools were likely to select less demanding coursework and to have lower academic self-concepts, lower GPAs, lower educational aspirations, and lower occupational aspirations in both their sophomore and senior years of high school. Attending higher-ability schools also negatively affected standardised test scores in the senior year of high school and subsequent college attendance, although these effects were smaller. For many senior year and post-secondary outcomes, there were statistically significant negative effects of school-average ability beyond those that could be explained in terms of sophomore outcomes. This implies that there are new, additional negative effects of school-average ability during the last two years of high school beyond the already substantial negative effects found early in high school. These results are consistent with previous research but are more compelling, important and remarkable because of the High School and Beyond's large sample size, diversity of academic outcomes, and longitudinal nature.

It is important to evaluate the effect of school-average ability after controlling for SES and academic ability. Whereas a disproportionate number of high-achieving students come from higher-ability schools, it is also apparent that a substantial proportion of students attending such schools are not achieving academic outcomes commensurate with their initial academic ability. Using an input-output analogy, the value added by higher-ability schools is negative compared to that of the lower-ability schools. Thus, the academic outcomes produced by higher-ability schools are not as good overall as would be expected on the basis of the quality of students who attend these schools. It is also important, however, to emphasise that the sizes of these negative effects of school-average ability are typically small and represent an average across 1000 high schools and many thousands of students. Hence, there will be some higher-ability schools that produce academic outcomes commensurate with the quality of their higher-ability students, and some students will be advantaged by attending such higher-ability schools. Nevertheless, it is unjustified to assume that higher-ability schools necessarily will advantage students. Attending higher-ability schools apparently disadvantages many students.

Do these effects generalise to 'gifted-and-talented' classes?

Most BFLPE research is based on de-facto selection processes that result in naturally occurring differences between schools and classes in terms of school- or class-average achievement. Extending this research, we (Marsh, Chessor *et al.*, 1995) designed two studies to test BFLPE predictions about the effects of participation in full-time 'gifted-and-talented' primary school classes. In both studies, students from gifted and talented programmes were matched to students of equal ability from mixed-ability classes. In both studies, students in the gifted-and-talented programme experienced significant declines in all three domains of academic self-concept. These declines were evident in comparisons over time based on students in gifted-and-talented classes over time and in relation to matched comparison students in mixed-ability classes. In both studies this general pattern of results was reasonably consistent across gender, age, and initial ability. A critical feature of these studies was a multidimensional perspective of self-concept. Consistent with *a priori* predictions based on theory and previous research, participation in gifted and talented programmes had a negative effect on academic self-concept and little or no effect on non-academic self-concept. This

prediction is important because most previous gifted-and-talented research was based on a unidimensional perspective of self-concept and relied on a single self-concept score that confounded differences between academic and non-academic self-concept. Hence, BFLPE research calls into question the assumed benefits of attending full-time gifted-and-talented classes and academically selective high schools.

Fall of the Berlin Wall: Quasi-experimental intervention to test the BFLPE

It seems unlikely that there will ever be a large-scale BFLPE study based on true random assignment. For this reason there is always potential for confounding the effects of academically selective schools and the characteristics of students who attend these schools. Such a situation, although always worrisome, is not as serious in BFLPE studies as in most research because the direction of any probable bias is in the opposite direction to BFLPE predictions. After controlling for initial ability, students in lower-ability schools tend to have higher academic self-concepts despite the fact that uncontrolled characteristics of the students or schools would be expected to favour selective school settings.

In one study, however, we (Marsh, Köller & Baumert, 2001) were able to evaluate the BFLPEs based on a quasi-experimental intervention – the fall of the Berlin Wall and the reunification of East and West Germany. Whereas I am not claiming that the fall of the Berlin Wall was designed to test the BFLPE it provided an ideal setting for comparing the effects of attending school systems that differed substantially in terms of the extent to which schools were differentiated according to ability.

In 1991, East and West German students experienced a remarkable social experiment in which the very different school systems of the former East Germany and West Germany were reunified following the fall of the Berlin Wall. This research was part of a large longitudinal project designed to evaluate the implications of the reunification of the two school systems conducted by the Max Planck Institute for Human Development. Prior to the reunification, the former East German system differed from the former West German system and the newly reunified system in two ways that were particularly important to social comparison processes in the formation of academic self-concept. First, the former East German students had explicitly not been grouped into schools or classes according to their achievement levels whereas the former West German students had attended schools based largely on their achievement levels for the previous two years. Second, the former East German system placed considerably more emphasis on highly competitive, social comparison processes that were likely to undermine academic self-concept. Hence, the self-concepts of former East German students were predicted to be lower overall than those of the former West German students. Immediately following the reunification, all German students attended schools grouped according to ability levels – largely adopting the West German school system.

In analysing this data, we (Marsh, Köller & Baumert, 2001) began by replicating the basic BFLPE results. Across all students, individual student achievement based on the standardised mathematics test had a positive effect on math self-concept (standardised path coefficient of 0.34) whereas class-average math achievement had a negative effect on math self-concept (–0.17). The most important new feature of this study was the comparison of results for different region (East vs. West Germany). Consistently with predictions based on school policies emphasising social comparison and a unitary system in the former East German school system, East German T1 math self-concepts were significantly lower than those of West German students (–0.11).

Of particular relevance, and also consistent with *a priori* predictions, there was a statistically significant interaction between region and class-average achievement; the BFLPE at the start of the first year after the reunification was more negative for West German students (who had already been tracked according to achievement in the previous two years) than for East German students (who were attending academically differentiated schools for the first time). Consistent with BFLPE predictions and the history of selective schooling in East and West Germany, however, the BFLPE was significantly bigger for West than East German students at the start of the reunification. Importantly, also consistent with predictions, the size of this difference was significantly smaller by the middle of the school year and had disappeared completely by the end of the first year of the reunified school systems. Results of this large-scale, quasi-experimental study clearly support the BFLPE and demonstrate how system-wide educational policy differences can impact on the academic self-concepts of individual students (Marsh, Köller & Baumert, 2001).

History may view the reunification of East and West Germany as one of the most important social interventions in the 20th century; certainly these effects were particularly profound for the German education system. Based on these cultural differences in the two school systems, we predicted what differences in the formation of academic self-concept would exist at the onset of the intervention and how these differences would change over the first year of the reunification into a single system based primarily on the West German model. The results of this research replicate a growing body of BFLPE research, conducted primarily in English-speaking countries, showing that academically selective educational programmes have negative effects on academic self-concept. The results are also important in: (a) providing strong support for the external validity of the BFLPE in a country where English is not the first language; (b) extending BFLPE research by showing how theoretical predictions vary consistently and logically in two groups (East and West German students) in a large-scale, quasi-experimental study; and (c) demonstrating how system-wide educational policy differences at the system level can impact on the academic self-concepts of individual students.

Juxtaposing counterbalancing (negative) contrast and (positive) reflected glory effects

BFLPE research has focused primarily on negative contrast effects – the negative effect of school- or class-average achievement. However, in the theoretical model underpinning this research (Marsh, 1984; also see Marsh & Craven, 2002) the BFLPE is hypothesised to be the net effect of two counterbalancing processes: (1) negative contrast effects that have been the focus of most research; and, (2) positive, reflected-glory, assimilation effects. Because the BFLPE is consistently negative, the negative contrast effect is apparently much stronger than the positive assimilation effect. Although reflected-glory assimilation effects have a clear theoretical basis, these effects have been implicit and have not been adequately operationalised in BFLPE studies.

To address this issue we (Marsh, Kong & Hau, 2000) employed a four-year longitudinal study to evaluate the BFLPE and the juxtaposition between assimilation and contrast effects for a large cohort of high schools in Hong Kong. Testing the generalisability of the BFLPE in Hong Kong is very interesting because the culture is different to the Western settings that are the basis of most BFLPE studies. On the one hand, Hong Kong is the most highly achievement segregated high school system in the world, which might be expected to lead to more negative contrast effects (i.e. the contextual differences are larger). On the other hand, because Chinese culture is low on individualism and high on collectivism, Chinese students should be less susceptible to the negative contrast effects due to social comparison processes and should have a

greater tendency to value their social group than students in more individualistic countries. Consistently with this perspective, 'face' – one's reputation and that of one's family – is of great concern in the Chinese culture, and admission to a prestigious high school is highly valued in Hong Kong. Hence, the gain in status and face for oneself and one's family due to attending a prestigious high school (reflected glory, assimilation) may possibly overshadow the loss in academic self-concept due to negative contrast resulting from comparisons with high achieving classmates. Also consistently with this potential de-emphasis of social comparison processes, Hong Kong students attribute their examination results more to effort than to ability, and concentrate more on their own improvement over time than on comparison with other students as determinants of perceived academic achievement. If Chinese students do value being members of academically selective schools (stronger assimilation effects) and their collective orientation reduces attention to social comparison processes (weaker contrast effects), the net BFLPE may be substantially less negative or close to zero.

The study was based on a large representative sample (7997 students from 44 high schools) of Hong Kong schools. Measures considered in this study were pretest achievement (T0Ach, scores on standardised tests administered prior to the start of high school for all Hong Kong students; the basis of admission into all high schools), standardised achievement tests administered at T1 (Year 7, T1Ach), T2 (Year 8, T2Ach), and T3 (Year 9, T3Ach), academic self-concept collected at T2 and T3 (T2ASC, T3ASC – based on a Chinese translation of the SDQII), and a measure of perceived school status (e.g. 'My school has a good reputation', 'The academic standard of my school is high, many students want to get in'). In preliminary results, we found that the effect of individual achievement was positive ($\beta = 0.34$ for Grade 8, .39 for Grade 9) whereas the effect of school-average achievement was negative (β = −0.20 for Grade 8, −0.22 for Grade 9). Although comparisons of beta-weights from different studies should be made cautiously, the sizes of these negative effects were comparable to those found in nationally representative samples of U.S. students (e.g. −0.21, Marsh, 1987; −0.23, Marsh, 1991).

In a series of multilevel regression models, we then juxtaposed predictions of the negative (contrast) effects of school-average ability on academic self-concept and the positive (assimilation, reflected glory) effects of school status on academic self-concept. The negative contrast effect was reflected in the negative effect of school average pretest achievement on academic self-concept after controlling at least individual pretest achievement (T0Ach). In the first set of models, the negative effect of school-average achievement on T2 academic self-concept varied from −0.22 (when only T0Ach was controlled) to −0.24 (when T0Ach, T1Ach, and T2Ach were controlled). This replicates the negative (contrast) effect found in many other BFLPE studies. Because academic self-concept was measured on two occasions, it was possible to evaluate the additional negative effects of school-average achievement at T3 beyond the negative effects at T2. These were models of self-concept change because the effects of T2 self-concept were partialled out of T3 self-concept. Not surprisingly, the largest effect on T3 self-concept was T2 academic self-concept, although individual academic achievement continued to have a positive effect. Of critical importance, the negative (contrast) effect of school-average achievement on T3 academic self-concept was still significantly negative even after controlling for the negative effect of school-average achievement mediated by T2 self-concept. Hence, there were new, additional negative effects of school-average achievement on T3 academic self-concept beyond the negative effects at T2. In summary, the Marsh, Kong and Hau (2000) results provide clear support for the negative

BFLPE in Hong Kong high schools. Not only were there negative BFLPEs for T2 and T3 academic self-concept considered separately, but the negative BFLPEs for T3 academic self-concept were larger than those that can be explained by the negative BFLPE already experienced at T2.

In subsequent analyses, we (Marsh *et al.*, 2000) modelled perceived school status as a function of prior achievement, academic self-concept, and school-average achievement. Perceived status was substantially a function of the school-average ability levels of students attending the school (effects of 0.56 to 0.60). Interestingly, we found that individual student achievement had a negative effect on perceived school status; better students perceived the status of their school to be lower than did poorer students. Furthermore, the negative effect of student achievement on school status was more negative when school-average achievement was low. This pattern of results is logical and consistent with our interpretation of reflected glory effects. Very high performing students performed better than most of the other students in their school – particularly if school-average achievement was low – so they did not experience as much 'reflected glory' as did students not doing as well who could 'look up to' the best students. Consistently with Buunk and Ybema's (1997) identification-contrast model, when students perceived themselves as being more able than their classmates there was little benefit in identifying with them. A more effective strategy, at least in terms of maximising academic self-concept, was to contrast their relatively superior skills with the weaker skills of their classmates. However, when students perceived their academic skills to be weaker than those of their classmates, it was a more effective strategy to identify with the high-perceived status of the school rather than to contrast their poorer skills with the superior skills of their classmates.

We (Marsh *et al.*, 2000) also added students' perceived status of their school to models of T3 academic self-concept. The critical features of these models were the juxtaposition of the effects of school-average achievement in models that included school status with those in corresponding models that did not include school status. The effect of perceived school status on T3 academic self-concept was positive (0.17) and continued to be positive even after controlling for T2 self-concept. Of critical importance, the effects of school-average achievement on T3 academic self-concept were substantially more negative (−0.33 and −0.31) in these models than in corresponding models that did not include school status. Thus, for example, in corresponding models that differed only in the inclusion of school status, the negative effect of school-average achievement was −0.33 when school status was included but only −0.23 when school status was excluded. The negative effect of school-average ability was consistently more negative when school status was included in each of the different models that were considered. In summary, the juxtaposition of the positive reflected glory assimilation effects of school status and the negative contrast effects of school-average achievement supported a priori predictions. Furthermore, the inclusion of school status into models of academic self-concept was consistent with *a priori* predictions, resulting in the negative effects of school-average achievement becoming more negative. These suppression effects were consistent with theoretical predictions that the BFLPE is a net effect of the positive assimilation and negative contrast effects. Hence, when the positive assimilation effects are controlled by the inclusion of school status, the negative effect of school-average achievement becomes a more pure measure of the negative contrast effects and school-average achievement effects become more negative.

More clearly than any previous BFLPE research, this study was able to differentiate between the negative social comparison contrast effects and the positive reflected glory assimilation effects that comprise the BFLPE. Whereas this finding is consistent with theoretical predictions and is implicit in previous explanations of the BFLPE, previous research has not operationalised the reflected glory effect. The results of this study imply that attending a school where school-average achievement is high simultaneously results in a more demanding basis of comparison for students within the school to compare their own accomplishments (the negative contrast effects) and a source of pride for students within the school (the positive reflected glory, assimilation effects). By including a separate measure of perceived school status, Marsh *et al.* (2000) partialled out some of the reflected glory effects associated with school-average achievement so that school-average achievement became a better (less confounded) basis for inferring social comparison contrast effects, leading to a more negative BFLPE. These results also imply that previous research may have underestimated the size of the negative contrast effects.

What are the implications for academically disadvantaged students?

The movement towards the inclusion of academically disadvantaged students into regular classrooms is a contentious issue which has generated many debates. Labelling theory suggests that placing academically disadvantaged students in special classes with other low-achieving students will lead to lower self-concepts and create a long lasting stigmatisation. On the basis of this theoretical argument there has been widespread support for the practice of integrating academically disadvantaged students into regular classrooms (i.e. 'mainstreaming'). In contrast, predictions based on BFLPE research imply that academically disadvantaged students will have higher self-concepts when grouped with other academically disadvantaged students (compared to similarly disadvantaged students in regular classroom settings).

Particularly relevant to this issue, Chapman's (1988) meta-analysis compared 'learning disabled' (LD) students who were:

(a) completely segregated in special classes; (b) partially segregated for some work and partially integrated in regular classes with non-LD students; and (c) 'unplaced' in completely integrated settings (i.e. LD students in regular classes who were not receiving LD remedial assistance). Whereas LD children in all three settings had poorer self-concepts than did non-LD children, the setting did make a difference. For general self-concept, students in fully segregated and partially segregated settings did not differ from each other but had better self-concepts than did unplaced LD students in regular classrooms. For academic self-concept, fully segregated children had higher self-concepts than partially segregated students and both groups had substantially better self-concepts than unplaced LD students. The decrement associated with being an unplaced LD student in regular classrooms was substantially larger for academic self-concept than for general self-concept. These results support social comparison theory and the BFLPE, but are complicated by the potential confounding between the type of setting and the amount of special assistance LD students received in the different settings. LD students apparently have substantially lower self-concepts than do non-LD students, and these deficits were particularly large for academic self-concept. These deficits, however, were substantially reduced if LD students were placed in fully segregated classes with other LD students. There was clear evidence that this strategy increased the academic self-concepts of LD students and there was no evidence to suggest that this strategy had any systematic effect on academic achievement. These results are important because they support social comparison theory and contradict predictions from labelling theory that have been used to argue against segregated classes.

In research leading to her PhD, Danielle Tracey (Tracey, 2002; Tracey, Marsh & Craven, 2003; Marsh, Tracey & Craven, 2006) more fully tested labelling and BFLPE predictions in a study of children with mild intellectual disabilities (IM). Because of the problems with measuring self-concept for this population experienced in previous research, we adapted the individualised administration approach developed by Marsh *et al.* (1991, 1998) which had been so successful with students as young as five years of age (see earlier discussion). The 211 IM students enrolled in Grades 2 to 6 had previously been identified as having a mild intellectual disability (i.e. an IQ of 56 to 75). On the basis of the students' current educational placement, we compared the self-concepts of IM students who were enrolled in regular mainstream classes with those enrolled in special IM classes.

Consistently with BFLPE predictions, students in special IM classes had significantly higher self-concepts for all three academic scales (see Figure 14; reading, math, school). In addition, however, these IM students had significantly higher peer self-concepts and significantly higher general self-concepts. The two groups did not differ significantly for the remaining three non-academic self-concepts (parents, physical Ability, physical appearance). In a subsequent qualitative component of the research, IM students in both educational placements were clearly aware that they were different from other students. Whereas these differences tended to alienate them from other students when all students did things together (e.g. recess), IM students in special classes felt more accepted by other students in their class than did IM students in mainstream regular classes. Hence, contrary to much of the rhetoric of the inclusion movement, IM students included in regular mainstream classes felt excluded, not included.

It should be noted that the results reported by Tracey and colleagues are based upon a cross-sectional design in which two intact groups are directly compared. Although potential counter-explanations based on non-equivalent groups are always worrisome, the direction of such a bias is

Figure 14: The negative effects on multiple dimensions of self–concept of placing students with mild intellectual disabilities (IM) in regular, mainstream classes compared to placing these students in special education classes.

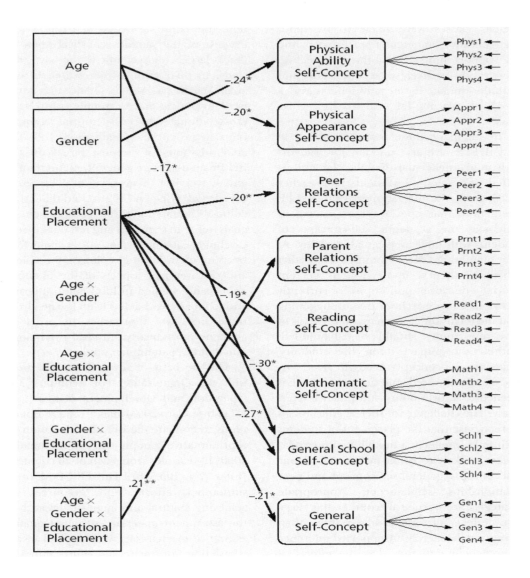

likely to run counter to predictions of social comparison theory. Hence, to the extent that there were pre-existing differences between the two groups, IM students in regular classes were likely to be more academically competent than those in the IM support units. From this perspective, these results are likely to be conservative and to underestimate the negative effects associated with placing IM students in regular classes.

In summary, these results demonstrate that BFLPEs are also relevant for students with mild intellectual disability (as well as gifted and talented students; see earlier discussion). Results support the BFLPE prediction that special class placement enhances the academic self-concepts of students with mild intellectual disability. At the same time these findings contradict labelling theory—upon which current special education philosophy is currently based. In this research we are not suggesting that the inclusion movement, on the basis of this one study, should be abandoned. Rather, the impact upon the students' academic self-concepts needs to be recognised and addressed, and further research is needed to inform policy and practice effectively. The challenge for special educators is to recognise that the placement of students with mild intellectual disability into regular classes is likely to result in lower academic self-concepts, general self-concept and peer relationships self-concept. Appropriate strategies are needed to counter this negative effect of inclusion, rather than accepting the largely unsupported inference from labelling theory that the effects of inclusion on self-concept are positive.

How specific are BFLPEs to particular cultural settings? Cross-cultural comparison across 26 countries

Early research demonstrating the BFLPE was conducted primarily in Western countries and, typically, in those where the native language is English. Whereas a growing number of studies have found support for the BFLPE model in different countries and cultural groups, each was based on results from a single country and a methodology (e.g. achievement indicators, instrumentation, translation, selection and representativeness of the sample, statistical analysis) that is largely idiosyncratic to the particular study. In their critique of research in this area, Marsh and Yeung (1999) noted the need to pursue more carefully constructed cross-national and cross-cultural comparisons in order to evaluate more fully the generalisability of support based on the BFLPE model. More generally, in their influential overview of cross-cultural research, Segall *et al.* (1998, p.1102) stated that cross-cultural research's three complementary goals were: 'to transport and test our current psychological knowledge and perspectives by using them in other cultures; to explore and discover new aspects of the phenomenon being studied in local cultural terms; and to integrate what has been learned from these first two approaches in order to generate more nearly universal psychology, one that has pan-human validity.'

On the basis of my collaborative work with the Organisation For Economic Co-Operation and Development (OECD), we (Marsh & Hau, 2003) had a unique opportunity to evaluate the BFLPE with nationally representative samples of approximately 4000, 15-year olds from each of 26 countries (total N = 103,558). The OECD devoted substantial efforts and resources to achieving cultural and linguistic breadth in the assessment materials, stringent quality-assurance mechanisms were applied in the translation of materials into different languages, and data were collected under independently supervised test conditions. As part of this process, items from the SDQII self-concept instrument were selected for inclusion in the research.

Consistently with the BFLPE, our initial results showed that the effects of school-average achievement (see Table 2) were negative in all 26 countries (M = –0.20, SD = 0.08). In order to clarify the extent of this

Table 2: Summary of multilevel models of the Big-Fish-Little-Pond effect (negative effect of school-average achievement) applied separately to each country (103,558 students; 3849 schools; 26 countries).

Country	Number of Students	Number of Schools	Intra-school Correlation for Achieve	Effects of (in prediction of Academic Self–concept)			
				Reliability Academic Self-concept	Individual Student Achieve	Individual Student Achieve^2	School Avg Achieve (BFLPE)
1 Australia	4916	223	0.17*	0.74	0.28*	0.05*	−0.15*
2 Austria	4444	163	0.45*	0.77	0.40*	0.08*	−0.15*
3 Belgium	3715	119	0.48*	0.70	0.14*	0.04*	−0.08*
4 Brazil	4015	258	0.35*	0.73	0.35*	0.06*	−0.17*
5 Czech Republic	4785	189	0.41*	0.77	0.40*	0.03*	−0.16*
6 Denmark	3973	199	0.10*	0.80	0.48*	0.07*	−0.11*
7 Finland	4768	153	0.06*	0.84	0.52*	0.11*	−0.09*
8 Germany	4815	208	0.52*	0.78	0.38*	0.06*	−0.20*
9 Hungary	4526	147	0.53*	0.72	0.27*	0.09*	−0.03
10 Iceland	2991	83	0.07*	0.81	0.63*	0.08*	−0.12*
11 Ireland	3785	136	0.14*	0.77	0.39*	0.03*	−0.16*
12 Italy	4931	163	0.45*	0.74	0.43*	0.04*	−0.24*
13 Korea	4913	134	0.37*	0.78	0.41*	0.13*	−0.01
14 Latvia	3552	128	0.26*	0.66	0.33*	0.04*	−0.04*
15 Liechtenstein	297	9	0.48*	0.76	0.27*	0.03	−0.13*
16 Luxembourg	3009	24	0.30*	0.74	0.32*	0.06*	−0.11*
17 Mexico	4231	158	0.46*	0.70	0.32*	0.07*	−0.05*
18 Netherlands	2480	100	0.47*	0.76	0.26*	0.05*	−0.17*
19 New Zealand	3473	152	0.16*	0.79	0.39	0.11	−0.17*
20 Norway	3863	162	0.08*	0.84	0.62*	0.09*	−0.12*
21 Portugal	4528	147	0.33*	0.73	0.42	0.08	−0.12*
22 Russia	6316	217	0.34*	0.72	0.46*	0.05*	−0.14*
23 Sweden	4325	149	0.09*	0.81	0.42*	0.07*	−0.22*
24 Switzerland	5522	213	0.37*	0.74	0.26*	0.06*	−0.11*
25 United Kingdom	2264	89	0.30*	0.74	0.28*	0.07*	−0.15*
26 United States	3121	126	0.27*	0.78	0.45*	0.04*	−0.17*
Mean	3983	148	0.31	0.76	0.38	0.07	−0.13
Median	4123	150	0.34	0.76	0.39	0.06	−0.14
SD	1190	57	0.16	0.04	0.11	0.03	0.06

Note: Ind Ach = Individual student achievement (linear component); Individual student achievement^2 = Squared Individual student achievement (quadratic component); School Avg Ach (BFLPE) = School-average achievement (the big-fish-little-pond effect, shown in **bold**). Adapted with permission from Marsh and Hau (2003).
* $p < 0.05$

country-to-country variation in the BFLPE, we conducted separate tests of the BFLPE for each of the 26 countries (see Table 1 and Figure 15). The effect of school-average achievement was significantly negative in 24 of 26 countries and non-significantly negative in the remaining two countries. The effect of school-average achievement was not positive in any of the 26 countries. Our study is particularly important, because it is clearly the largest and strongest cross-cultural test of the BFLPE, demonstrating the generalisability of the theoretical and empirical basis of our claim.

Summary: Big-Fish-Little-Pond effect

BFLPE research provides an alternative, contradictory perspective to educational policy on the placement of students in special education settings; a policy that is being enacted throughout the world. Remarkably, despite the very different issues, this clash between our research and much existing policy is found at both ends of the achievement continuum (also see Robinson, Zeigler & Gallagher, 2000). In gifted education research and policy, there is an increasing trend toward the provision of highly segregated educational settings – special Gifted-and-Talented classes and academically selective schools for very bright students. This policy direction is based in part on a labelling theory perspective, suggesting that bright students will have higher self-concepts and experience other psychological benefits from being educated in the company of other academically gifted students. Yet, our BFLPE and empirical evaluation of the effects of academically selective settings show exactly the opposite effects. Placement of gifted students in academically selective settings results in lower academic self-concepts, not higher academic self-concepts.

In recent research and policy for academically disadvantaged students, there is a worldwide inclusion movement to integrate these students into mainstream, regular classroom settings. Although economic rationalist perspectives appear to be the underlying motive for such decisions, the espoused rhetoric is based on a direct application of labelling theory. According to labelling theory, academically disadvantaged children are likely to be stigmatised and suffer lower self-concepts as a consequence of being placed in special classes with other academically disadvantaged students. Yet, theory underpinning our BFLPE and empirical evaluation of the effects of including academically disadvantaged students in regular mainstream classrooms show exactly the opposite effects. Placement of academically disadvantaged children into regular classrooms results in lower academic self-concepts, not higher academic self-concepts. Furthermore, the negative effects of inclusion on peer self-concept reported by Tracey *et al.* (2003), suggested that academically disadvantaged children in regular classrooms actually felt socially excluded, not included.

We do not claim that all Gifted-and-Talented students will suffer lower academic self-concepts when attending academically selective high schools, but many will. Similarly, we do not claim that all academically disadvantaged students will suffer lower academic self-concepts when attending regular, mixed-ability classes, but many will. Rather, our research provides an important alternative perspective to existing policy directions that have not been adequately evaluated in relation to current educational and psychological research. The present investigation is particularly important in demonstrating the cross-cultural generalisability of the theoretical and empirical basis of our claims.

Figure 15: The big-fish-little-pond effect from a multilevel perspective.

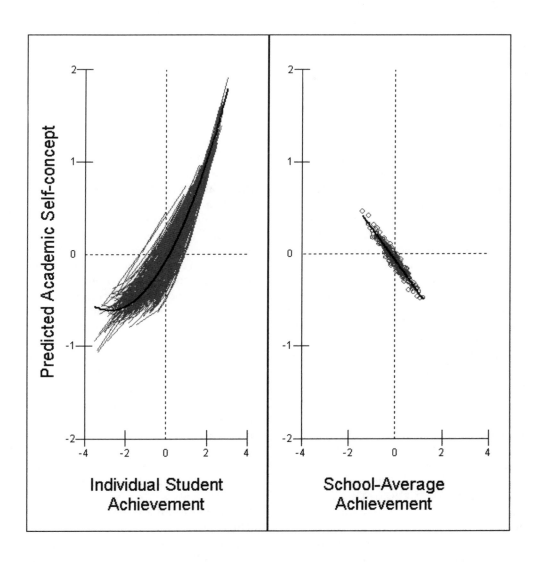

(A) Individual Student Achievement. Each of the lines (in gray) represents the relation between achievement and self-concept in a particular school. The solid line is averaged across all schools. (B) School-Average Achievement. The scatter plot of points (in gray) represents the relation between school-average achievement and self-concept (i.e. each point represents a single school. The solid (dark) line is the regression equation across all schools.

Herbert W. Marsh

Intervention studies: Need for a multidimensional perspective

The enhancement of self-concept is an important goal in many disciplines and a means to facilitate other desirable outcomes (Craven *et al.*, 2003). Acknowledgement of the importance of self-concept has led to a proliferation of self-concept enhancement intervention research. However, traditional literature reviews have been unable to either elucidate or test promising directions in the self-concept enhancement literature because of its sheer volume and because of the apparently atheoretical, contradictory nature of the literature (Marsh & Craven, 1997). A variety of research practices have been used in the self-concept enhancement literature, making comparisons across studies difficult. Furthermore, many of the older studies are based on outdated theoretical models, weak research designs, and poor measurement instruments (Hattie, 1992), and have not capitalised on recent advances in theory and research (Craven *et al.*, 2003; Marsh & Hattie, 1996; Marsh, 1993a, 1990a).

A multidimensional, construct validity approach

An important advance in methodology has been the construct validity approach to the study of self-concept intervention effects (Marsh & Craven, 1997). This construct validity approach suggests that interventions should be evaluated as to their impact on: (a) specific facets of self-concept directly related to the goals of the intervention; (b) facets closely related to the target facets; and (c) self-concept facets that are unrelated to the goals of the intervention (see Marsh & Craven, 1997; Marsh, 1993a). According to a multidimensional perspective of self-concept, interventions should impact in ways that map onto specific, relevant dimensions of the self-concept. Hence, intervention studies provide a strong test of the construct validity of a multidimensional

perspective of self-concept. To the extent that an intervention has the predicted pattern of effects on multiple dimensions of self-concept, there is even stronger support for the construct validity of interpretations of the intervention. I have identified this approach to intervention design and evaluation in a number of different studies.

Physical fitness enhancement

Marsh and Peart (1988) randomly assigned high school students to competitive, cooperative and control groups. The cooperative group completed exercises in pairs; feedback emphasised individual improvement. The competitive/social comparison group completed individual exercises; feedback emphasised comparisons with whoever did best on each exercise. Consistently with a priori predictions it was found that the cooperative intervention increased physical fitness and physical self-concept; the competitive intervention increased physical fitness but decreased physical self-concept. Importantly for a multidimensional perspective, the intervention effects were specific to physical components of self-concept; global self-esteem and other non-physical components of self-concept were unaffected.

Outward bound studies

The construct validity approach was demonstrated in a series of studies based on the Outward Bound programme, which encourages individuals to recognise and understand their own weaknesses, strengths, and resources and thus find within themselves the wherewithal to master the difficult and the unfamiliar.

The Outward Bound standard course is a 26-day residential programme based on physically and mentally demanding outdoor activities (Marsh, Richards & Barnes, 1986a, 1986b). The authors evaluated short- and long-term effects of participation in the Outward Bound programme using the SDQIII. Prior to the start of the study, the programme Director rated the relevance of each of the 13 SDQIII scales to the goals of the programme. Results were consistent with the primarily non-academic goals of the Outward Bound standard course: (a) gains were significantly larger for the SDQIII scales predicted *a priori* to be most relevant to the goals of the programme; (b) the effect sizes were consistent across 27 different Outward Bound groups run by different instructors at different times and in different locations; and (c) the size and pattern of the gains were maintained over an 18-month follow-up period.

In contrast to the Outward Bound standard course, the Outward Bound bridging course is a six-week residential programme designed to produce significant gains in the academic domain for underachieving adolescent males through an integrated programme of remedial teaching, normal schoolwork and experiences likely to influence academic self-concept (Marsh & Richards, 1988). Consistently with the primarily academic goals of the Outward Bound bridging course: (a) academic self-concept effects were substantial and significantly larger than non-academic self-concept effects; and (b) there were also corresponding effects on reading and math achievement.

The juxtaposition of these two interventions and support for their contrasting predictions provides a powerful demonstration of the importance of a multidimensional perspective of self-concept. If only these studies had only measured global self-esteem, both interventions would have been judged much weaker, and a rich understanding of the match between specific intended goals and actual outcomes would have been lost.

A meta-analysis approach to self-concept interventions

Haney and Durlak (1998) performed a meta-analysis on 99 self-concept intervention studies conducted prior to 1992 for children and adolescents under the age of 18. They sought to elucidate: whether interventions led to significant improvements in self-concept; whether improvements in self-concept were associated with other desirable outcomes; and to distinguish any factors that moderated outcome success. Of particular note, treatments found to be specifically focused on self-concept enhancement (i.e. target studies; mean effect size = 0.57) were significantly more effective than treatments focused on other aspects, such as social skills (0.10). They also reported that studies using prior empirical evidence to inform their design had greater effect sizes (0.71) than those with theoretical bases (0.50) and those with no strong rationale (0.12). In terms of the design of the intervention itself, Haney and Durlak found that treatment programmes exhibited greater change (0.47) than prevention studies (0.09). Non-randomised designs resulted in significantly lower effect sizes (0.04) than randomised studies (0.38). Studies with no treatment control groups had significantly higher effect sizes (0.34) than studies with attention-placebo controls (0.10). And, like Hattie (1992), Haney and Durlak found that only five of the 120 interventions they analysed reported follow-up data for self-concept, making long-term effectiveness difficult to gauge. Importantly, based on these results Haney and Durlak (1998, p.429) concluded, 'it is possible to significantly improve children's and adolescents' levels of SE/SC and to obtain concomitant positive changes in other areas of adjustment. There is even the suggestion that SE/SC [self-esteem and self-concept enhancement] programmes do at least as well as other types of interventions in changing other domains. Haney and Durlak also suggested that significant improvements in self-concept are unlikely unless interventions focus on self-concept. This suggestion is supported by the longitudinal causal modelling studies discussed earlier, which demonstrated that the strongest effect on subsequent self-concept is prior self-concept.

Haney and Durlak's (1998) meta-analysis makes an important contribution to self-concept enhancement research. We note, however, that they argued that (p.424) 'there is also no agreement about whether SE/SC is best conceptualised in unidimensional, multidimensional, or hierarchical terms.' Consistently with this perspective, when more than one factor of self-concept score was considered within a given study, they took an average of these scores so that there was only one effect size per study. This approach is also consistent with typical practice in meta-analytic research, in which multiple outcomes from the same study are averaged to form a single outcome per study, thus avoiding statistical problems (violations of assumptions of independence). In contrast, we argue that it is important to distinguish between the effects of an intervention on target areas of self-concept that are directly relevant to the goals of the programme (e.g. math self-concept for a math intervention), the effects of an intervention on related areas of self-concept where one might predict a transfer effect (e.g. academic self-concept for a math intervention), and the effects of an intervention on non-target areas (e.g. physical self-concept for a math intervention). Based on self-concept theory and empirical research (e.g. Marsh & Craven, 1997), as well as common sense, target effects should be substantially larger than non-target effects.

In order to pursue this issue in greater detail, O'Mara, Marsh *et al.* (2006) conducted a new meta-analysis of self-concept enhancement studies. They extended previous meta-analyses by including studies published up to 2002 (Haney & Durlak, 1998, was based on studies published prior to 1992). However, the major difference to the previous meta-analyses was an emphasis on the multidimensionality of self-concept. Thus, a separate effect size was computed for each self-concept outcome considered in the study. The different components of self-concept were then classified as being directly related, indirectly related, or unrelated to the intervention. Despite considering nearly two-thirds more studies than the Haney and Durlak meta-analysis, the O'Mara *et al.* results largely replicated those of the earlier meta-analysis. However, consistently with *a priori* hypotheses, the new meta-analysis results showed that effect sizes were substantially larger for self-concept scales that were directly related to the intervention and substantially smaller for those components of self-concept that were not. These results indicated that the Haney and Durlak meta-analysis substantially underestimated the effect of self-concept interventions – particularly those studies that specifically operationalised a multidimensional perspective of self-concept. Consistently with a growing body of research, the O'Mara *et al.* meta-analysis provides strong support for a multidimensional perspective of self-concept and argues against an ongoing reliance on the unidimensional perspective.

O'Mara *et al.* (2006) concluded that the application of sophisticated meta-analytic techniques to evaluate self-concept intervention studies has proved to be valuable for synthesising and critically analysing the available body of self-concept intervention studies. The mean effect size of 0.51 means that children and adolescents are benefiting from self-concept enhancement interventions. Further, the findings point to new ways in which we can improve self-concept interventions. For example, more effective interventions incorporated appropriate praise and/or feedback strategies into the programme, especially strategies that are contingent upon performance, attributional in nature, and goal-relevant. The authors also indicated that targeting children and adolescents with diagnosed problems may be more valuable than instigating preventive programmes. However, the most important new finding was in regard to the multidimensionality of self-concept. The results suggest that interventions need to focus on specific dimensions of self-concept and then assess the effects of the intervention in relation to that particular self-concept domain instead of, or in addition to, other specific and global components of self-concept. Rather than using generic, non-specific interventions that try to improve all aspects of the children's and adolescents' self-evaluations at once, researchers should focus on domain specific programmes to ensure the goals of the programmes are truly met. In terms of programme evaluation, using multi-dimensional measures is important because the results of their meta-analysis indicate that using global scales of self-concept may underestimate intervention benefits. As a result, it is possible that successful intervention features have not been detected because inadequate scales cannot detect significant gains resulting from the treatments. Given the importance of having a positive self-concept, and the money and time invested into implementing enhancement programmes, it seems timely for researchers and practitioners to capitalise on developments in multidimensional self-concept theory and instrumentation to create an array of interventions that target domain specific facets of self-concept.

Herbert W. Marsh

New applications of self-concept research

Self-concept is an exciting construct that is applicable to almost all research involving human beings. Underlying much self-concept research is the assumption that individuals with higher self-concepts feel better about themselves and that this leads to more effective performance and other desirable outcomes. Support for this assumption is particularly strong in educational research, but can be easily translated to many other areas of applied research. In collaboration with PhD students and colleagues around the world, I am currently undertaking a range of new applied studies that are hoped to result in significant implications for theory, policy and practice.

Bullies, victims, violence and aggression

Bullying, violence, and victimisation in schools are pervasive problems with long-term psychological consequences for bullies, victims and communities. Anti-bullying programmes, although popular internationally, are rarely developed to capitalise on recent theoretical advances and systematically analysed by rigorous research. Grounded on cutting edge research in anti-bullying, school ethos, self-concept and cognitive psychology, we developed an innovative whole-school anti-bullying intervention for high school students. In his PhD thesis, Parada (2006; Parada, Craven & Marsh, 2003; also see Marsh, Parada *et al.*, 2004) we critically evaluated its impact on desirable social and educational outcomes for victims, bullies, and other students using a powerful multi-cohort-multi-occasion experimental design and state-of-the-art quantitative and qualitative analyses, tracking both individual students and whole schools over time.

One of the first studies to come from this new research project evaluates the pivotal role of self-concept in relation to bullying (Marsh, Parada *et al.*, 2001). Aggressive troublemaking and being a victim were related to three components of self-concept (general, same sex, and opposite sex) based on the large, nationally representative NELS database. Longitudinal structural equation models for students in Grades 8, 10 and 12 showed that the troublemaker and victim constructs were reasonably stable over time and, importantly, moderately correlated (many students were both troublemakers and victims). The victim factor was negatively correlated with self-concepts and had negative effects on subsequent self-concepts. Whereas the troublemaker factor was also correlated somewhat negatively with self-concepts, the troublemaker factor had small positive effects on subsequent self-concept. This suggests, interestingly, that low self-concept may trigger troublemaking behaviour in a possibly successful attempt to enhance subsequent self-concept. Although boys had higher troublemaker and victim scores than girls, the effects of these constructs on subsequent self-concepts were similar for boys and girls. The results indicate that bullies derive a sense of self-worth from their anti-social activities and suggest that this may be reinforced by others. Hence, an effective means to undermine bullying behaviours may be to alter the social ethos within a school that reinforces bullying behaviours.

We (Marsh, Parada *et al.*, 2004) posed three provocative questions with important implications for future research and policy, and provided some tentative answers based on our research.

● Are bullies and victims more alike than different?

There are some obvious differences between bullies and victims, but what may be more surprising is the similarity between bullies and victims on a wide variety of psychological constructs such as: attitudes toward bullying, roles taken on when confronted with a bullying situation, strategies for coping with problems, inability to control anger, depression, life event stress, low self-concept on most of the different areas of self-concept measured, and global self esteem. These similarities seem surprising from a historical, bipolar perspective of bullies and victims, whereby being a bully and being a victim have been assumed to be bipolar opposites. However, our research showed that bullies tend to be victims of bullying, and victims tend to be bullies. Furthermore, our causal modelling also revealed support for a reciprocal effects model; previous bullying leads to subsequently being bullied, whereas previously being bullied leads to subsequently being a bully. Thus, when results are interpreted from the fresh perspective of our reciprocal effects model, it is not surprising that bullies and victims are similar on a variety of psychological constructs.

- Do low self-concepts and depression lead to being victimised or are these merely by-products of being a victim?

Our results provide reasonably clear evidence that low self-concepts and high levels of depression do lead to being a victim. Thus, positive self-perceptions provide a strategic approach to developing psychological tools and resiliency that serve to protect students from becoming victims. However, by drawing upon our reciprocal effects model, our results also extend these findings by demonstrating that these positive self-perceptions also protect students from becoming bullies.

- Do school bullies successfully use bullying behaviours as a strategy to enhance their self-concepts and reduce depression?

Our results provide reasonably clear evidence that there are no benefits to being a bully in terms of increased levels of self-concept or lowered levels of depression. However, even if the use of bullying for this purpose is not a successful strategy, it is still possible that it remains a motivation for students to become bullies. For this reason, it is important that the school community of students, teachers, administrators, and parents reinforces the unacceptability of bullying behaviours so that students cannot delude themselves into thinking that such socially inappropriate behaviours can result in enhanced social status and self-perceptions – real or self-perceived.

Our research also has some potentially important implications for interventions. Bullies have particularly low self-concepts on the honesty/trustworthy, parent relationships, and school scales. This suggests that interventions aimed at building moral values associated with home and school may provide a deterrent to bullying behaviours. Interestingly, these are three of the self-concept scales where victims scored higher than bullies. In contrast, victims had lower self-concepts than bullies, particularly on the two peer-relationship scales. This supports interventions designed to improve the social skills of victims in particular. Whereas both bullies and victims were low on anger control, victims tended to internalise anger, whereas bullies tended to externalise it. Bullies, but also, and more particularly victims, tended to use avoidance to deal with potentially stressful situations. Thus, anger control and effective coping strategies may be an important ingredient in intervention programmes. Whereas both bullies and victims tended to be depressed, victims were much more depressed than bullies. Finally, a successful intervention must be able to alter the pattern of positive pro-bully and negative pro-victim attitudes held by bullies.

Self-concept, peer support and the peer support foundation

School-based peer support programmes are very popular and are seen to provide important benefits in educational settings throughout the world. Such programmes, however, are rarely evaluated systematically using a strong research design, a suitable range of outcome measures and a dual focus on both the junior students (tutee) and senior students (tutor). Of particular interest is the effect of peer support programmes on the potentially stressful transition from primary to secondary schools that is associated with declines in attendance, academic achievement and self-concept, and increases in classroom misbehaviour and depressive symptoms. Evidence also indicates that those who do not successfully negotiate the transition are at increased risk of long-term problems including school failure, premature school drop-out, and serious forms of emotional dysfunction during adult life. It is, therefore, important to find out whether peer support programmes can counter these negative effects. Since peer support plays an important role in adolescent adjustment, it is important to explore whether peer support programmes lead to an increase in perceived social support by students in the programme and a strong sense of 'connectedness' with the school. The results of this study should have profound effects for our conceptual understandings of the key strengths of peer support programmes and their benefits for high school participants.

In her recent PhD thesis Louise Ellis (2005; also see Ellis, Marsh & Craven, 2005) sought to explicate these issues by employing a sound research design to examine the effectiveness of a widely-used secondary school peer support programme based on new and existing psychometrically sound measurement instruments. In this research she sought to evaluate the effects of the programme for both younger students (tutees) and older students who did the tutoring. The results of Study 1 demonstrated that instruments employed in her thesis were psychometrically sound for high school students. Study 2 showed that that the programme was largely successful in achieving its stated aims of enhancing Year 7 students' school self-concept, school citizenship, sense of self, connectedness, resourcefulness and sense of possibility for the future. Study 3 of the thesis revealed that the programme also led to a variety of benefits for the peer support leaders, including enhancements in leadership ability, school citizenship and peer relations. In Study 4

Ellis used qualitative findings to enrich the quantitative results of Studies 2 and 3, and to provide valuable insights into the ways in which the programme could be improved in the future. Her findings have important implications for the provision of programmes and techniques employed to address students' problems following the transition to adolescence and secondary school, and for the successful implementation of peer support programmes.

De-institutionalisation of people with mild intellectual disabilities

In her PhD thesis on the integration of long-term institutionalised adults into the mainstream community, Rose Dixon (2005; also see Dixon, Marsh & Craven, 2004) compared changes over time for a group of long-term institutionalised women who were integrated back into the community (movers) with a second group of adults who remained in an institutional setting (stayers) in terms of social competence and affective development (self-concept, self esteem and locus of control). Whereas de-institutionalisation is potentially beneficial, there is also evidence that as a consequence of this de-institutionalisation many people lead lonely, isolated and socially restricted lives. The thesis employed a unique combination of complementary qualitative and quantitative research methodologies and an interpersonal cognitive problem-solving intervention. In Study 1, the impact of the quasi-experimental intervention on multidimensional measures of self-concept, locus of control, quality of life and adaptive behaviour demonstrated a reasonably consistent pattern of results amongst the difference constructs. In particular, there were no advantages gained by remaining in the institution and the advantages of de-institutionalisation were exhibited in some facets of self-concept, some domains of quality of life and in some areas of adaptive behaviour.

Study 2 used a case-study approach to explore the social competency and self-esteem of a subset of the movers from

Study 1. A lack of socialisation experiences was the primary reason for the lack of social competencies and skills exhibited by the participants, which also had an impact on their self-esteem. The participants' self-esteem improved when they moved into the community, thus supporting a stigma or labelling theory. Finally, the third study reports on the design and implementation of an intervention to increase the social skills of people with intellectual disabilities, whose community placement was considered to be vulnerable because they exhibited challenging behaviours. It used a single subject multiple baseline methodology across pairs of subjects, to assess the impact of a social cognitive problem-solving technique on improving challenging social skills where the emphasis was on generalisation to the community and maintenance over time and generalisation to real-life social behaviours. Target behaviours chosen for intervention were idiosyncratic to each participant because of the nature of their disabilities.

These findings have important implications for current theories of self-concept, people with intellectual disabilities, the provision of programmes and techniques to improve self-concept, and also for the provision of social skills programmes to enhance the social competencies and hence, the social integration of people who have been deinstitutionalised.

Obesity, body image, and self-concept: Actual–ideal discrepancy models

The increasing prevalence of childhood obesity throughout the developed world has drawn much public attention. Motivating obese children to participate in regular exercise, and hence to prevent obesity, can however be difficult (e.g. Marsh, Papaioannou & Theodorakis, 2006; Pierce & Wardle, 1997). Obese children are more prone to low self-esteem (Braet, Mervielde & Vandereycken, 1997; Pierce & Wardle, 1997; Johnson, 2002). In related research, Crandall (1991) reviewed research showing that

individuals are discriminated against on the basis of weight, that this discrimination generalises over race, gender, age, and socioeconomic status, and that the associated stigmatisation influences the individual's self-perceptions and perceptions by significant others. However, much of this research relating self-concept to body composition has adopted an implicit unidimensional perspective that emphasises self-esteem – a single, global domain of self-concept – rather than a multidimensional perspective that emphasises multiple, relatively distinct components of self-concept (Marsh, Craven & Martin, in press; Marsh & Craven, 2006) that are more strongly related to relevant outcomes in diverse disciplines. Particularly in sport and exercise psychology, researchers have increasingly focused on multidimensional measures specifically designed to reflect different components of physical self-concept (Fox & Corbin, 1989; Marsh, 1997, 2002; Sonstroem, 1997) rather than – or in addition to – self-esteem.

Discrepancy theory: Actual and ideal body image

Frame of reference effects considered thus far have focused on evaluation of one's own accomplishments in relation to those of others (social comparison) or in relation to one's own academic accomplishments in one school subject with one's own accomplishments in other school subjects. Here I look at a qualitatively different sort of frame of reference, the ideal standards that one establishes as an appropriate outcome. In psychology there is a long history of research relating actual self-concept ratings (how one actually is), ideal self-concept ratings (how one ideally would like to be), global self-esteem, and other, more specific components of self-concept. Historically, theories about ideal and actual perceptions and their relations to self-concept stem from heuristic speculations arising from William James' oft-cited quote about the shame of being second best when one aspires to be best, leading him to conclude that objective accomplishments are evaluated in relation to internal frames of reference: 'we have the paradox of a man shamed to death because he is only the second pugilist or the second oarsman in the world' (James, 1890, p.310). Following James, the relations between global esteem and self-perceptions in a specific domain (e.g. physical, social, academic) typically are posited to depend on individual standards or ideals for the specific domain.

Whereas James did not operationalise these constructs nor pursue empirical tests of his hypotheses, Wells and Maxwell (1976; also see Wylie, 1974) reviewed discrepancy approaches in which self-esteem is predicted to depend on the discrepancy between actual and ideal self-perceptions. Favourable self-perceptions in a specific domain should contribute positively to esteem, but high or unrealistic ideals (i.e. ideals that are difficult or impossible to achieve) in the specific domain should contribute negatively. However, these early reviews of the discrepancy approach to self-esteem were also very critical of the many problems associated with the use of simple difference scores, and more recent reviews (e.g. Hattie, 1992; Marsh, 1993a; Pelham & Swann, 1989) continue to provide only limited support for the usefulness of discrepancy scores based on the difference between actual and ideal self-concept ratings. One reason for this typical failure of the actual–ideal discrepancy model may be an ambiguity in the ideal rating task previously identified by Wylie (1974). For most domains the ideal naturally falls at the positive end of the rating scale such that, all other things being equal, it is better to be smart, popular, good looking, rich, athletic, healthy, etc. For this reason there is not much variation in ideal ratings and that variation which does exist is likely to be idiosyncratic, suspect, or random error. Hence most studies have found that actual–ideal discrepancies are less correlated with global self-esteem and other criterion variables than actual ratings alone.

Silhouette matching task and discrepancy theory

In the silhouette matching task (SMT; see Figure 16) individuals are presented with a set of silhouette drawings varying from very thin to very obese and, for example, asked to choose the silhouette that is most like them (actual self), the one they would most like to look like (ideal self), or any of a variety of other questions that can be keyed to this pictorial response scale (e.g., Hallinan, Pierce, Evans, DeGrenier & Andres, 1991; Marsh, 1999; Marsh & Roche, 1996; Tiggemann, 1992). SMT studies typically have focused on gender differences, or on differences between "normals" and clinical samples. Thus, for example, compared to males, females tend to have larger actual–ideal discrepancies and to have ideal-self scores that are thinner than their actual-self scores (Tiggemann, 1992; also see Cash, Morrow *et al.*, 2004; Feingold & Mazzella, 1998).

The underlying thin-fat continuum and the SMT have several advantages that make them well-suited for testing actual–ideal discrepancy models. For example, the "pictorial" response scale on the SMT is better anchored to the underlying thin-fat continuum than the potentially ambiguous – and value-laden – verbal labels in typical Likert response scales. Of particular relevance to tests of the actual–ideal discrepancy model, ideal ratings are likely to fall somewhere in the middle of the thin-fat continuum rather than on one or the other of the endpoints. Hence, there is reasonable variation in ideal ratings as well as the actual ratings, and it is possible to have positive and negative discrepancies.

Marsh and Roche (1996) devised new tests of discrepancy theory based on silhouette ratings. Students selected one of a number of silhouettes that varied on a thin-obese continuum to represent their actual body image (what I actually look like today) and ideal body image (what I would ideally like to look like). Actual silhouette ratings were substantially correlated ($r = 0.62$) with

Figure 16: Silhouette Matching Task.

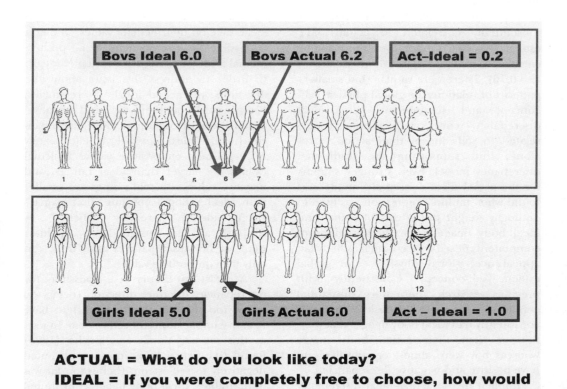

ACTUAL = What do you look like today?

IDEAL = If you were completely free to choose, how would you ideally like to look?

Respondents respond to each question (e.g. What do you look like today?) by choosing the appropriate silhouette.

objective body composition (BMIs, girths, and skinfolds). Whereas body fat self-concept on the PSDQ instrument was substantially correlated to actual SMT ratings ($r = 0.66$), it was even more highly correlated with actual–ideal discrepancies ($r = 0.76$). There were similar (but smaller) patterns of relations for global physical self-concept and self-esteem. Actual–ideal discrepancy scores were more strongly related to self-concept than actual scores alone, thus supporting the traditional discrepancy model. Even stronger support for the actual–ideal discrepancy model was found when multiple regression was used to optimally weight the effects of actual and ideal body image in predicting different components of self-concept such as body fat, appearance, global physical, and global esteem self-concept. Consistently with previous research, there were substantial gender differences in this task in that girls consistently had ideal body images that were thinner than their actual body image whereas boy were almost equally likely to have positive and negative discrepancies.

Implicit in the actual–ideal discrepancy model is the assumption that actual–ideal discrepancies can only be negative; that discrepancies reflect a failure to realise ideal standards. In the case of the SMT this translated into predictions that ideal ratings would be thinner than actual ratings, so that actual ratings would contribute negatively to self-concept (the more obese one is, the lower one's self-concept), and ideal ratings would contribute positively (the heavier one's ideal standards, the easier it is to obtain one's ideal and, thus, achieve a higher self-concept). Thus, actual–ideal discrepancies should be positive, and the larger these discrepancies, the more negative that self-concepts are expected to be. This rationale may be reasonable for many areas where the ideal logically corresponds to one or the other endpoint. Whereas it might be possible to actually exceed one's ideal, this would typically be a particularly positive outcome that would contribute posi-

tively to self-esteem. However, Marsh and Roche (1996) argue that this logic might be dubious in areas like body image, in which ideals take on intermediate values, so that it is possible for discrepancies to be positive (actual > ideal) or negative (actual < ideal). In order to address this issue about the direction of actual–ideal discrepancies, I distinguish between raw and absolute actual–ideal discrepancies. Raw discrepancies [actual– ideal, hereafter labelled as raw A-I] can take on positive values if actual ratings are larger than ideal ratings, and negative values if actual ratings are smaller than ideal ratings. Absolute discrepancies (|actual–ideal|, hereafter labelled as Abs|A-I|) are the unsigned (or absolute) value of raw discrepancies and, thus, can only take on positive values.

At least in theory it is possible for discrepancies in either direction (being too fat or too thin relative to ideals) to have negative implications for self-esteem. In tests of this model, Marsh and Roche (1996) found that actual body image contributed negatively to self-esteem (being too fat was undesirable), ideal body image contributed positively (having fatter, more realistic ideal self-concepts led to higher self-esteem), and having small absolute discrepancies between actual and ideal body image contributed positively. In their results based upon Australian adolescents, it was clearly negative to be too fat relative to one's ideals, but it was also undesirable (to a much lesser extent) to be too thin.

In recent research with the SMT, Marsh, Hall *et al.* (in press) tested the extent to which their results based on Western (Australian) adolescents generalised to Chinese children and adolescents. They especially focused on cultural differences in the pattern of results from Chinese students compared to typical Western findings in which there are systematic, gender stereotypic differences in multiple dimensions of self-concept and an apparent preoccupation with thinness – particularly for girls. In their review of body dissatisfaction research for

Chinese students they argued that there was less drive for thinness and that traditionally fuller figures were seen to reflect health and prosperity. Also, based on the Chinese doctrine of the mean, which emphasises moderation and a reasonable middle path between extremes, Marsh et al. suggested that it was reasonable for Chinese students to seek a body image that is neither too fat nor too thin. Whereas previous research (e.g. Marsh & Roche, 1996) found that it was mostly negative discrepancies (actual body image much fatter than ideal body image) that contributed to low self-esteem, the doctrine of the mean suggests that both positive and negative discrepancies (being too fat or too thin relative to ideals) will contribute to lower self-esteem for Chinese participants.

Marsh, Hau et al. (in press) began by 'translating' the SMT into Chinese – using pictorial representations of Chinese children rather than the Western figures used by Marsh and colleagues. We then related multiple dimensions of physical self-concept, SMT ratings of actual and ideal body image, and objective measures of body composition for Chinese children aged 8 to 15 ($N = 763$), and compared the results to Western research. Compared to Western research, gender differences favouring boys were generally much smaller for Hong Kong students across physical self-concept factors, and particularly SMT ratings of body image. Objective and subjective indexes of body fat were negatively related to many components of physical self-concept, but – in contrast to Western research – were unrelated to global self-esteem and slightly positively related to health self-concept. In support of discrepancy theory, actual–ideal discrepancies in body image were related to physical self-concept. However, consistently with the Chinese cultural value of moderation, and in contrast to Western results, being too thin relative to personal ideals was almost as detrimental as being too fat. Although the Chinese students were somewhat younger and included a wider age range than did the Australian sample, the results in both cultural samples were reasonably independent of age.

The Marsh, Hall et al. (in press) results support the usefulness of responses to the PSDQ and SMT ratings in obesity research, and the multidimensional perspective to self-concept that underpins our research. Although there are many similarities between Chinese and Australian results, there were some important differences consistent with a priori predictions based on cultural differences between Chinese and Western cultures, which have important theoretical and practical implications. In particular, Australian children – particularly girls – apparently place more emphasis on being thin, and this has a substantial effect on their self-concepts, including self-esteem. In contrast, Hong Kong children place less emphasis on being thin, and body image has less impact on their self-concepts and none at all on self-esteem. Indeed, for Chinese students obesity was almost unrelated to self-esteem and somewhat positively related to health self-concept. Especially Australian girls have ideal body images that are much thinner than Australian boys, whereas Chinese girls have somewhat fatter ideal body images than Chinese boys. These results reflect Chinese cultural values in which obesity is apparently more acceptable than in Western culture, and, perhaps, general inadequacies of health education about the health risks associated with obesity. It will, however, be interesting to see if this situation changes as awareness of obesity as a health problem becomes stronger in China, as government policy is implemented to address this problem, and, perhaps, as China becomes more 'Westernised' in increasingly adopting the value of thinness.

Summary and implications

Interest in self-concept stems from its recognition as a valued outcome, from its assumed role as a moderator variable, from interest in its relation with other constructs, and from interest in related methodological and measurement issues. Historically, self-concept research has been noted for a lack of rigor in its theoretical models and measurement instruments. Even though important within-construct issues such as the dimensionality of self-concept had not yet been resolved, the majority of self-concept research focused on the relation between self-concept and other constructs. Early in my research programme I took the position that theory, measurement, and good research are inexorably intertwined; each will suffer if any of these components is ignored. Research described here supports the construct validity of responses to SDQ instruments and the Shavelson *et al.* model upon which they are based. The research has also clarified many theoretical issues in self-concept research and led to a revision of the Shavelson *et al.* model. In this sense SDQ research represents an interplay between theory and empirical research, and supports the construct validity approach that guided SDQ research. Based on my early research, the strongest contribution may be the development of instruments, based on strong empirical and theoretical foundations, for the measurement of multiple dimensions of self-concept. This solid foundation has allowed me to pursue important substantive, theoretical, and policy-oriented issues that otherwise would not have been possible. Several of these overarching directions of my subsequent research have been highlighted here.

A central theme of the review was the multidimensionality of self-concept. Historically, self-concept research has emphasised a global dimension of self. More recent research, such as described here, emphasises specific dimensions of self and may call into question the usefulness of a general dimension of self. Marsh *et al.* (1988) similarly concluded that academic self-concept cannot be understood adequately if specific dimensions of academic self-concept are ignored, suggesting that at least verbal and mathematical components of self should be considered. Marsh and Shavelson (1985) concluded that self-concept cannot be understood adequately if its multidimensionality is ignored. The further substantiation of this conclusion has been the major thrust of this presentation. This was a major theme of our (Marsh & Craven, 2006) critique of the Baumeister *et al.* (2003, 2005) reviews and has been a critical feature in nearly all of my self-concept publications.

My research has increasingly led to the conclusion that general self-concept – no matter how it is inferred – may not be a particularly useful construct in educational psychology. Shavelson *et al.* (1976) initially hypothesised that general self-concept should be the most stable facet in their hierarchy. The general self-concept scale on SDQ instruments, however, tends to be one of the least stable scales. Similarly, the general school scale is less stable than more specific domains of academic self-concept, even though its internal consistency is high. The findings suggest that these more general domains – at least as they are reflected in global scales typically used to measure general self-concept – are more affected by short-term response biases, short-term mood fluctuations, and other short-term time-specific influences. General self-concept apparently cannot adequately reflect the diversity of specific self domains. If the role of self-concept research is to better understand the complexity of self in different contexts, to predict a wide variety of behaviours, to provide outcome measures for diverse interventions, and to relate self-concept to other constructs, then the specific domains of self-concept are more useful than a general domain.

Particularly in educational settings, the separation of academic from non-academic and general domains of self-concept provides important support for this contention. Interestingly, work leading to the Marsh/Shavelson revision suggests that these criticisms of an over-reliance on general self-concept also apply to the usefulness of a general academic self-concept. Because math and verbal self-concepts are nearly uncorrelated, they cannot be adequately explained by a general academic self-concept. I am not arguing that researchers should abandon measures of general self-concept and general academic self-concept, but rather that more emphasis needs to be placed on content-specific dimensions of self-concept. Researchers should be encouraged to consider multiple dimensions of self-concept particularly relevant to the concerns of their research, supplemented, perhaps, by more general measures. Likewise, teachers need to be encouraged to utilise multidimensional assessment instruments rather than unidimensional assessment instruments that solely measure global measures of self-concept. Self-concept enhancement should target specific facets of self-concept rather than the common practice of targeting general self-concept. For example, if a child has a low reading self-concept the most direct means of enhancing this facet of self-concept is by directly targeting it rather than general self-concept. Further support for these recommendations comes from the evaluation of studies that relate general and content-specific dimensions of self-concept to other constructs (see Marsh, 1990c) and relations involving educationally relevant outcomes that are the focus of the research summarised here.

A significant theme highlighted here was that a positive self-concept is important, in part, because it facilitates other desirable accomplishments. Hence, research looking at the reciprocal effects between academic self-concept and academic outcomes – and the REM – has been an important topic. The results of this research clearly supports REM predictions that academic self-concept and achievement are each a cause and an effect of the other, and reject older models claiming that linkages were either from achievement to self-concept or from self-concept to achievement. Support for the REM in educational settings also has important implications for classroom teachers who need to focus on simultaneously enhancing both achievement and self-concept. Interesting new research suggests that the REM can be appropriately applied to other domains such as elite and non-elite sport, and physical health. Because self-esteem is typically almost uncorrelated with academic achievement, we argue that it is not a particularly useful measure in tests of the REM in educational settings. The combination of my multidimensional perspective and REM was the basis of integrating pessimistic conclusions by Baumeister *et al.* (2003, 2005) about the effects of positive self-esteem with our optimistic conclusions about the effects of academic self-concept in educational settings.

However, I have not considered in detail the extensive range of studies that relate self-esteem to a wide variety of other variables. In arguing for the importance of a multidimensional perspective, we do not argue, as apparently do Baumeister *et al.* (2003, 2005), that there are no positive consequences associated with having a positive self-esteem. Rather our claim is that the effects of specific components of self-concept most logically related to the outcomes are stronger than those of self-esteem in educational settings. Indeed, many (e.g. Branden, 1994; Sommer & Baumeister, 2002; Trzesniewski *et al.*, 2006) argue that there exists an extensive literature, spanning diverse disciplines and theoretical perspectives, suggesting that high self-esteem promotes goals, expectancies, coping mechanisms, and behaviours that facilitate productive achievement and work experiences, and impede mental and physical health problems, substance abuse, and anti-social behaviour. Even the most strident critics of overgeneralisations based on self-esteem (e.g. Baumeister *et al.*, 2003, 2005) concede that a positive self-esteem may promote a sense of happiness. Using a prospective, longitudinal design based on a large birth cohort study, Trzesniewski *et al.* (2006) reported that adolescents with low self-esteem subsequently (10 years later) had poorer mental and physical health, worse economic prospects (more likely to leave school early and to have money problems; less likely to attend university), and higher levels of criminal behaviour during adulthood, compared to adolescents with high self-esteem – even after controlling for adolescent depression, gender, socioeconomic status, IQ, and body mass index. Furthermore, the pattern was similar for outcome measures based on objective measures and informant self-reports. Hence, they argued that low self-esteem during adolescence predicts negative real-world consequences during adulthood. However, recognising that many of the effect sizes were modest, they concluded that low adolescent self-esteem was one of many potentially modifiable risk factors for a wide variety of adult adjustment problems. Hence I contend that it is premature to conclude that self-esteem results in mere 'seductive pleasure', as suggested by Baumeister *et al.* (2003).

Another general theme highlighted in the present overview is the effect of frames of reference. Self-concept depends on self-perceptions of one's own strengths and weaknesses and the frame of reference used to evaluate these self-perceptions. The BFLPE demonstrated that the accomplishments of others in one's immediate environment provide an important frame of reference inherent in social comparison processes. Furthermore, the frame of reference established by the academic skills of others is quite specific to academic self-concept. The internal comparison process in the I/E model demonstrated that one's relative accomplishments in one sphere may

also serve as a frame of reference for evaluating accomplishments in other areas. The Marsh and Peart (1988) study also suggested that some potentially powerful interventions that enhance skill levels may have a negative effect on self-concept because the gains in skills are more than offset by changes in frames of reference used to evaluation self-perceptions of the skill levels. Particularly our more recent cross-cultural comparisons based on the PISA data with both the I/E model (Marsh & Hau, 2004) and the BFLPE (Marsh & Hau, 2003) demonstrate the broad generalisability of predictions based on these theoretical models.

An additional theme has been the developmental processes in the formation and the convergence of self-concept responses and external validity criteria. Our research (see review by Marsh, Debus & Bornholt, 2005) suggests that we are able to measure multiple dimensions of self-concept at a younger age than previously thought possible. Our research also shows that at least during early pre-adolescent years self-concept appears to become more differentiated with age. Whereas there is clear evidence of increasing differentiation among facets of self-concept as young children grow older, there is also support for increasing integration of closely related facets of self-concept as posited in the differential distinctiveness hypothesis (Marsh & Ayotte, 2003). During pre-adolescence and early adolescence self-concept declines systematically with age; I have attributed this trend to the perhaps unrealistically high self-concepts (at least in relation with external criteria) becoming increasingly realistic and reflecting the influence of external sources of information. Relations between academic self-concept and academic achievement were typically lower in preadolescence than in late adolescence. Self-other agreement was markedly stronger in late adolescence than pre-adolescence. As children grow older their self-concepts more accurately reflect information about self provided by external sources.

In my research programme I have tried to integrate: sound theory; solid measurement with strong psychometric properties; extensive research evidence; and substantive application with clear policy implications. This methodological/substantive synergy has been a repeated theme in my research programme. By seeking methodological solutions to real substantive problems, I have been able to build my methodological research in a way that would not have been possible if there had not been a strong substantive basis for the research. Likewise, my substantive research has benefited from the application of new, evolving methodological approaches to address questions that could not be adequately addressed with traditional methodologies. In my research programme I have developed a multimethod approach that is a systematic, natural extension of the construct validity approach that was the explicit basis of my self-concept research programme and of the original Shavelson *et al.* (1976) model (see Marsh *et al.*, 2006). Much of the logic from this multimethod perspective comes from MTMM analyses and the many advances in this approach to construct validation. The essence of the construct validity approach is to look for areas of convergence and nonconvergence in measures of the same construct across multiple methods. At the micro-level, the multiple 'methods' might be different items used to infer the same latent construct. At an intermediate level of abstraction, the multiple methods might be different instruments designed to measure similar constructs or responses from different individuals about the same target person (e.g. student, teacher, parent).

At a higher level of abstraction the multiple methods might be different constructs that are posited to be related (achievement and self-concepts in different school subjects) or fundamentally different research methodologies (e.g. qualitative and quantitative studies). In my research I have expanded this notion of multiple perspectives to include multilevel modelling to evaluate the extent of generalisability, for example, across different schools and across different countries. From this perspective I have viewed cross-cultural research as another application of multimethod research in which the multiple nationalities or cultures are seen as multiple methods to test the generalisability of measures, empirical results, and theoretical predictions. Whereas this diversity of multimethod applications is not easily encapsulated into neat multimethod taxonomy, the essence of the approach is to interrogate psychological research findings from multiple perspectives – multiple indicators, multiple outcomes, multiple independent variables, multiple methodologies, multiple analytical approaches, and multiple settings. The extent to which these multiple perspectives are incorporated into research designs impacts substantially on the construct validity of the results and the confidence with which conclusions can be generalised. Based on this integrative approach, I have attempted to show that theory, instrument development, research, and practice are all inextricably intertwined – perhaps providing a model for other research programmes in educational psychology as well as other disciplines of psychology and the social sciences.

References

Alwin, D.F. & Otto, L.B. (1977). High school context effects on aspirations. *Sociology of Education, 50,* 259–273.

Bachman, J.G. & O'Malley, P.M. (1977). Self-esteem in young men: A longitudinal analysis of the impact of educational and occupational attainment. *Journal of Personality and Social Psychology, 35,* 365–380.

Baumeister, R.F., Campbell, J.D., Krueger, J.I. & Vohs, K.D. (2003). Does high self-esteem cause better performance, interpersonal success, happiness, or healthier lifestyles? *Psychological Science in the Public Interest, 4,* 1–44.

Baumeister, R.F., Campbell, J.D., Krueger, J.I. & Vohs, K.E. (2005). Exploding the self-esteem myth. *Scientific American, 292,* 84–92.

Boyle, G.J. (1994). Self-Description Questionnaire II: A review. *Test Critiques, 10,* 632–643.

Braet, C., Mervielde, I. & Vandereycken, W. (1997). Psychological aspects of childhood obesity: A controlled study in a clinical and nonclinical sample. *Journal of Pediatric Psychology, 22,* 59–71.

Branden, N. (1994). *Six pillars of self-esteem.* New York: Bantam.

Brookover, W.B. (1989). *Self-Concept of Ability Scale – A review and further analysis.* Paper presented at the Annual Meeting of the American Educational Research Association.

Brookover, W.B. & Lezotte, L.W. (1979). *Changes in schools characteristics coincident with changes in student achievement.* East Lansing, MI: Michigan State University. (ERIC Document Reproduction Service No. ED 181 005).

Brown, J.D. (1993). Self-esteem and self-evaluation: Feeling is believing. In J. Suls (Ed.), *Psychological perspectives on the self* (Vol. 4, pp.27–58). Hillsdale, NJ: Erlbaum.

Buunk, B.P. & Ybema, J.F. (1997). Social comparisons and occupational stress: The identification-contrast model. In P.P. Buunk & F.X. Gibbons (Eds.), *Health, coping, and well-being: Perspectives from social comparison theory* (pp.359–388). Mahwah, NJ: Erlbaum.

Burns, R.B. (1982). *Self-concept development and education.* London: Holt, Rinehart & Winston.

Byrne, B.M. (1984). The general/academic self-concept nomological network: A review of construct validation research. *Review of Educational Research, 54,* 427-456.

Byrne, B.M. (1996a). Academic self-concept: Its structure, measurement, and relation to academic achievement. In B.A. Bracken (Ed.), *Handbook of self-concept* (pp.287–316). New York: Wiley.

Byrne, B.M. (1996b). *Measuring self-concept across the life span: Issues and instrumentation.* Washington, DC: American Psychological Association.

Calsyn, R. & Kenny, D. (1977). Self-concept of ability and perceived evaluations by others: Cause or effect of academic achievement? *Journal of Educational Psychology, 69,* 136–145.

Cash, T.F., Morrow, J.A., Hrabosky, J.I. & Perry, A.A. (2004). How has body image changed? A cross-sectional investigation of college women and men from 1983 to 2001. *Journal of Consulting & Clinical Psychology, 72,* 1081–1089.

Chapman, J.W. (1988). Learning disabled children's self-concepts. *Review of Educational Research, 58,* 347–371.

Chapman, J.W. & Tunmer, W.E. (1997). A longitudinal study of beginning reading achievement and reading self-concept. *British Journal of Educational Psychology, 67,* 279–291.

Coopersmith, S.A. (1967). *The antecedents of self-esteem.* San Francisco: W.H. Freeman.

Crain, R.M. (1996). The influence of age, race, and gender on child and adolescent multidimensional self-concept. In B.A. Bracken (Ed.), *Handbook of self-concept: Developmental, social, and clinical considerations* (pp.395–420). New York: Wiley.

Crandall, C.S. (1991). Do heavyweight students have more difficulty paying for college? *Personality and Social Psychology Bulletin, 17,* 606–611.

Craven, R.G., Marsh, H.W. & Burnett, P.C. (2003). Cracking the self-concept enhancement conundrum: A call and blueprint for the next generation of self-concept enhancement research. In H.W. Marsh, R.G. Craven & D.M. McInerney (Eds.), *International Advances in Self Research* (Vol. 1, pp.67-90). Greenwich, CT: Information Age.

Dai, D.Y. (2002). Incorporating parent perceptions: A replication and extension study of the internal-external frame of reference model of self-concept development. *Journal of Adolescent Research, 17,* 617–645.

Dai, D.Y. (2004). How universal is the big-fish-little-pond effect? *American Psychologist, 59,* 267–268.

Davis, J.A. (1966). The campus as a frog pond: An application of theory of relative deprivation to career decisions for college men. *American Journal of Sociology, 72,* 17–31.

Davis-Kean, P. & Sandler, H.M. (2001). A meta-analysis of measures of self-esteem for young children: A framework for future measures. *Child Development, 72,* 887–906.

Dixon, R. (2005). *Moving out: The impact of deinstitutionalising on salient affective variables, social competence and social skills of people with mild intellectual disabilities.* Unpublished PhD Thesis, University of Western Sydney (http://self.uws.edu.au/)

Dixon, R., Marsh, H.W. & Craven, R.G. (2004). *Moving out: The impact of deinstitutionalisation on salient affective variables, social competence and social skills for people with mild intellectual disabilities.* Paper presented at the Proceedings of the Third International Biennial SELF Research Conference, Berlin, Germany, 4–7 July.

Eccles, J., Wigfield, A., Harold, R.D. & Blumenfeld, P. (1993). Age and gender differences in children's self- and task perceptions during elementary school. *Child Development, 64,* 830–847.

Eder, R.A. & Mangelsdorf, S.C. (1997). The emotional basis of early personality development: Implications for the emergent self-concept. In R. Hogan, J.Johnson & S. Briggs (Eds.), *Handbook of personality psychology* (pp.209–240). San Diego, CA: Academic Press.

Ellis, L. (2005). *Peers helping peers: The effectiveness of a peer support programme in enhancing self-concept and other desirable outcomes.* Unpublished PhD Thesis, University of Western Sydney (http://self.uws.edu.au/).

Ellis, L.A., Marsh, H.W. & Craven, R.G. (2005). Navigating the transition to adolescence and secondary school: A critical evaluation of the impact of peer support. In H.W. Marsh, R.G. Craven & D. McInerney (Eds.), *New frontiers for self-research. International Advances in Self Research* (Vol. 2, pp.329–356). Greenwich, CT: Information Age Publishing.

Fantuzzo, J.W, McDermott, P.A., Manz, P.H., Hampton, V.R. & Burdick, N.A. (1996). The pictorial scale of perceived competence and social acceptance: Does it work with low-income urban children? *Child Development, 67,* 1071–1084.

Feingold, A. & Mazzella, R. (1998). Gender differences in body image are increasing. *Psychological Science, 9,* 190–195.

Festinger, L. (1954). A theory of social comparison processes. *Human Relations, 7,* 117–140.

Fleishman, F.A. (1964). *The structure and measurement of physical fitness.* Englewood Cliffs, NJ: Prentice-Hall.

Fox, K.R. & Corbin, C.B. (1989). The physical self-perception profile: development and preliminary validation. *Journal of Sport & Exercise Psychology, 11*(4), 408–430.

Gill, D.L., Dzewaltowski, D.A. & Deeter, T.E. (1988). The relationship of competitiveness and achievement orientation to participation in sport and nonsport activities. *Journal of Sport and Exercise Psychology, 10,* 139–150.

Guay, F., Marsh, H.W. & Boivin, M. (2003). Academic self-concept and academic achievement: Developmental perspectives on their causal ordering. *Journal of Educational Psychology, 95,* 124–136.

Hallinan, C.J., Pierce, E.F., Evans, J.E., DeGrenier, J.D. & Andres, F.F. (1991). Perceptions of current and ideal body shape of athletes and nonathletes. *Perceptual and Motor Skills, 72,* 125–130.

Haney, P. & Durlak, J.A. (1998). Changing self-esteem in children and adolescents: A meta-analytic review. *Journal Of Clinical Child Psychology, 27,* 423–433.

Hattie, J. (1992). *Self-concept.* Hillsdale, NJ: Erlbaum.

Helmke, A. & van Aken, M.A.G. (1995). The causal ordering of academic achievement and self-concept of ability during elementary school: A longitudinal study. *Journal of Educational Psychology, 87,* 624–637.

Helson, H. (1964). *Adaptation-level theory.* New York: Harper & Row.

Hyman, H. (1942). The psychology of subjective status. *Psychological Bulletin, 39,* 473–474.

James, W. (1890/1963). *The principles of psychology.* New York: Holt, Rinehart & Winston (original work published 1890).

Jerusalem, M. (1984). Reference group, learning environment and self-evaluations: A dynamic multi-level analysis with latent variables. In R. Schwarzer (Ed.), *The self in anxiety, stress and depression* (pp.61–73). North-Holland: Elsevier Science Publishers. .

Johnson, C. (2002). Obesity, weight management, and self-esteem. In T.A. Wadden & A.J. Stunkard (Eds.), *Handbook of obesity treatment* (pp.480–493). New York: Guilford Press.

Kagen, S.L., Moore, E. & Bredekamp, S. (1995). *Considering children's early development and learning: Toward common views and vocabulary* (Report N. 95-03). Washington, DC: National Education Goals Pane.

Kling, K.C., Hyde, J.S., Showers, C.J. & Buswell, B.N. (1999). Gender differences in self-esteem: A meta-analysis. *Psychological Bulletin, 125,* 470–500.

Marsh, H.W. (1974). *Judgmental anchoring: Stimulus and response variables.* Unpublished doctoral dissertation, University of California, Los Angeles.

Marsh, H.W. (1984). Self-concept: The application of a frame of reference model to explain paradoxical results. *Australian Journal of Education, 28,* 165–181.

Marsh, H.W. (1986). Verbal and math self-concepts: An internal/external frame of reference model. *American Educational Research Journal, 23,* 129–149.

Marsh, H.W. (1987). The hierarchical structure of self-concept and the application of hierarchical confirmatory factor analysis. *Journal of Educational Measurement, 24,* 17–19.

Marsh, H.W. (1989). Age and sex effects in multiple dimensions of self-concept: Preadolescence to Early-adulthood. *Journal of Educational Psychology, 81,* 417-430.

Marsh, H.W. (1990a). The causal ordering of academic self-concept and academic achievement: A multiwave, longitudinal panel analysis. *Journal of Educational Psychology, 82,* 646–656.

Marsh, H.W. (1990b). A multidimensional, hierarchical self-concept: Theoretical and empirical justification. *Educational Psychology Review, 2,* 77–172.

Marsh, H.W. (1990c). The structure of academic self-concept: The Marsh/Shavelson model. *Journal of Educational Psychology, 82,* 623–636.

Marsh, H.W. (1991). The failure of high ability high schools to deliver academic benefits: The importance of academic self-concept and educational aspirations. *American Educational Research Journal, 28,* 445–80.

Marsh, H.W. (1992). The content specificity of relations between academic achievement and academic self-concept. *Journal of Educational Psychology, 84,* 35–42.

Marsh, H.W. (1993a). Academic self-concept: Theory, measurement and research. In J. Suls (Ed.), *Psychological perspectives on the self* (Vol. 4, pp.59–98). Hillsdale, NJ: Erlbaum.

Marsh, H.W. (1993b). The multidimensional structure of academic self-concept: Invariance over gender and age. *American Educational Research Journal, 30,* 841–860.

Marsh, H.W. (1993c) The multidimensional structure of physical fitness: Invariance over gender and age. *Research Quarterly for Exercise and Sport, 64,* 256–273.

Marsh, H.W. (1994). Using the National Educational Longitudinal Study of 1988 to evaluate theoretical models of self-concept: The Self-Description Questionnaire. *Journal of Educational Psychology, 86,* 439–456.

Marsh, H.W. (1997). The measurement of physical self-concept: A construct validation approach. In K. Fox (Ed.), *The physical self-concept: From motivation to well-being* (pp.27–58). Champaign, IL: Human Kinetics.

Marsh, H.W. (1999). Cognitive discrepancy models: Actual, ideal, potential, and future self-perspectives of body image. *Social Cognition, 17*(1), 46–75.

Marsh, H.W. (2002). A multidimensional physical self-concept: A construct validity approach to theory, measurement, and research. *Psychology: The Journal of the Hellenic Psychological Society, 9,* 459–493.

Marsh, H.W. & Ayotte, V. (2003). Do multiple dimensions of self-concept become more differentiated with age? The differential distinctiveness hypothesis. *Journal of Educational Psychology, 95,* 687–706.

Marsh, H.W. & Byrne, B.M. (1991). Differentiated additive androgyny model: Relations between masculinity, femininity, and multiple dimensions of self-concept. *Journal of Personality & Social Psychology, 61,* 811–828.

Marsh, H.W. & Byrne, B.M. (1993). Do we see ourselves as others infer: A comparison of self-other agreement on multiple dimensions of self-concept from two continents. *Australian Journal of Psychology, 45,* 49–58.

Marsh, H.W., Byrne, B.M. & Shavelson, R. (1988). A multifaceted academic self-concept: Its hierarchical structure and its relation to academic achievement. *Journal of Educational Psychology, 80,* 366–380.

Marsh, H.W., Byrne, B.M. & Yeung, A.S. (1999). Causal ordering of academic self-concept and achievement: Reanalysis of a pioneering study and revised recommendations. *Educational Psychologist, 34,* 154–157.

Marsh, H.W., Chanal, J.P., Sarrazin, P.G. & Bois, J.E. (2006). Self-belief does make a difference: A reciprocal effects model of the causal ordering of physical self-concept and gymnastics performance. *Journal of Sport Sciences, 24,* 101–111.

Marsh, H.W., Chessor, D., Craven, R.G. & Roche, L. (1995). The effects of gifted-and-talented programmes on academic self-concept: The big fish strikes again. *American Educational Research Journal, 32,* 285–319.

Marsh, H.W. & Craven, R.G. (1991). Self-other agreement on multiple dimensions of preadolescent self-concept: The accuracy of inferences by teachers, mothers, and fathers. *Journal of Educational Psychology, 83,* 393–404.

Marsh, H.W. & Craven, R. (1997). Academic self-concept: Beyond the dustbowl. In G. Phye (Ed.), *Handbook of classroom assessment: Learning, achievement, and adjustment* (pp.131–198). Orlando, FL: Academic Press.

Marsh, H.W. & Craven, R.G. (2002). The pivotal role of frames of reference in academic self-concept formation: The Big-Fish-Little-Pond Effect. In F. Pajares & T. Urdan (Eds.), *Adolescence and Education* (Vol. II, pp.83–123). Greenwich, CT: Information Age Publishing.

Marsh, H.W. & Craven, R.G. (2006). Reciprocal effects of self-concept and performance from a multidimensional perspective. Beyond seductive pleasure and unidimensional perspectives. *Perspectives on Psychological Science, 1*(2), 133–163.

Marsh, H.W., Craven, R.G. & Debus, R. (1991). Self-concepts of young children aged 5 to 8: Their measurement and multidimensional structure. *Journal of Educational Psychology, 83,* 377–392.

Marsh, H.W., Craven, R.G. & Debus, R. (1998). Structure, stability, and development of young children's self-concepts: A multicohort-multioccasion study. *Child Development, 69,* 1030–1053.

Marsh, H.W., Craven, R.G. & Martin, A. (in press). What is the nature of self-esteem: Unidimensional and multidimensional perspectives. In M. Kernis (Ed.), *Self-esteem: Issues and Answers.* Psychology Press.

Marsh, H.W., Debus, R. & Bornholt, L. (2005). Validating young children's self-concept responses: Methodological ways and means to understand their responses. In D.M. Teti (Ed.), *Handbook of Research Methods in Developmental Science* (pp.138–160). Blackwell Publishers: Oxford, UK.

Marsh, H.W., Ellis, L. & Craven, R.G. (2002). How do pre-school children feel about themselves? Unravelling measurement and multidimensional self-concept structure. *Developmental Psychology, 38,* 376–393.

Marsh, H.W. & Hattie, J. (1996). Theoretical perspectives on the structure on self-concept. In B.A. Bracken (Ed.), *Handbook of self-concept* (pp.38–90). New York: Wiley.

Marsh, H.W. & Hau, K.T. (2003). Big-fish-little-pond effect on academic self-concept: A crosscultural (26 country) test of the negative effects of academically selective schools. *American Psychologist, 58,* 364–376.

Marsh, H.W. & Hau, K.T. (2004). Explaining paradoxical relations between academic self-concepts and achievements: Cross-cultural generalisability of the internal-external frame of reference predictions across 26 countries. *Journal of Educational Psychology, 96,* 56–67.

Marsh, H.W., Hau, K.T. & Kong, C.K. (2002). Multilevel causal ordering of academic self-concept and achievement: Influence of language of instruction (English compared with Chinese) for Hong Kong students. *American Educational Research Journal, 39,* 727–763.

Marsh, H.W., Hau, K.T., Sung, R.Y.T. & Yu, C.W. (in press). Childhood obesity, gender, actual–ideal body image discrepancies, and physical self-concept in Hong Kong children. *Developmental Psychology.*

Marsh, H.W. & Hocevar, D. (1985). The application of confirmatory factor analysis to the study of self-concept: First and higher order factor structures and their invariance across age groups. *Psychological Bulletin, 97,* 562–582.

Marsh, H.W., Köller, O. & Baumert, J. (2001). Reunification of East and West German school systems: Longitudinal multilevel modeling study of the big-fish-little-pond effect on academic self-concept. *American Educational Research Journal, 38*(2), 321–350.

Marsh, H.W. & Köller, O. (2003). Bringing together two theoretical models of relations between academic self-concept and achievement. In H.W. Marsh, R.G. Craven & D.M. McInerney (Eds.), *International Advances in Self Research* (Vol. 1, pp.17–48). Greenwich, CT: Information Age.

Marsh, H.W., Kong, C.K. & Hau, K.T. (2000). Longitudinal multilevel modelling of the Big-Fish-Little-Pond effect on academic self-concept: Counterbalancing social comparison and reflected glory effects in Hong Kong high schools. *Journal of Personality and Social Psychology, 78,* 337–349.

Marsh, H.W., Kong, C.K. & Hau, K.T. (2001). Extension of the internal/external frame of reference model of self-concept formation: Importance of native and nonnative languages for Chinese students. *Journal of Educational Psychology, 93*(3), 543–553.

Marsh, H.W., Martin, A.J. & Hau, K.T. (2006). A multiple method perspective on self-concept research in educational psychology: A construct validity approach. In M. Eid & E. Diener (Eds.), *Handbook of Multimethod Measurement in Psychology* (pp.441–456). American Psychological Association: Washington DC.

Marsh, H.W. & Myers, M.R. (1986). Masculinity, femininity, and androgyny: A methodological and theoretical critique. *Sex Roles, 14,* 397–430.

Marsh, H.W. & O' Neill, R. (1984). Self Description Questionnaire III (SDQ III): The construct validity of multidimensional self-concept ratings by late-adolescents. *Journal of Educational Measurement, 21,* 153–174.

Marsh, H.W., Papaioannou, A. & Theodorakis, Y. (2006). Causal ordering of physical self-concept and exercise behavior: Reciprocal effects model and the influence of physical education teachers. *Health Psychology, 25,* 316–328.

Marsh, H.W., Parada, R.H. & Ayotte, V. (2004). A multidimensional perspective of relations between self-concept (Self Description Questionnaire II) and adolescent mental health (Youth Self Report). *Psychological Assessment, 16,* 27–41.

Marsh, H.W., Parada, R.H., Craven, G.R. & Finger, L. (2004). In the looking glass: A reciprocal effects model elucidating the complex nature of bullying, psychological determinants and the central role of self-concept. In C.S. Sanders & G.D. Phye (Eds.), *Bullying: Implications for the classroom.* Orlando, FL: Academic Press.

Marsh, H.W., Parada, R.H., Yeung, A.S. & Healey, J. (2001). Aggressive school troublemakers and victims: A longitudinal model examining the pivotal role of self-concept. *Journal of Educational Psychology, 93*(2), 411–419.

Marsh, H.W. & Parker, J. (1984). Determinants of student self-concept: Is it better to be a relatively large fish in a small pond even if you don't learn to swim as well? *Journal of Personality and Social Psychology, 47,* 213–231.

Marsh, H.W. & Peart, N. (1988). Competitive and co-operative physical fitness training programmes for girls: Effects on physical fitness and on multidimensional self-concepts. *Journal of Sport and Exercise Psychology, 10,* 390–407.

Marsh, H.W. & Perry, C. (2005). Does a positive self-concept contribute to winning gold medals in elite swimming? The causal ordering of elite athlete self-concept and championship performances. *Journal of Sport and Exercise Psychology, 27,* 71–91.

Marsh, H.W. & Richards, G. (1988a). The Outward Bound Bridging Course for low achieving high-school males: Effect on academic achievement and multidimensional self-concepts. *Australian Journal of Psychology, 40,* 281–298.

Marsh, H.W., Richards, G. & Barnes, J. (1986a). Multidimensional self-concepts: A long-term follow-up of the effect of participation in an Outward Bound programme. *Personality and Social Psychology Bulletin, 12,* 475–492.

Marsh, H.W., Richards, G. & Barnes, J. (1986b). Multidimensional self-concepts: The effect of participation in an Outward Bound programme. *Journal of Personality and Social Psychology, 45,* 173–187.

Marsh, H.W., Richards, G.E., Johnson, S., Roche, L. & Tremayne, P. (1994). Physical Self-Description Questionnaire: Psychometric properties and a multitrait-multimethod analysis of relations to existing instruments. *Sport and Exercise Psychology, 16,* 270–305.

Marsh, H.W. & Roche, L.A. (1996). Predicting self-esteem from perceptions of actual and ideal ratings of body fatness: Is there only one ideal 'supermodel'? *Research Quarterly for Exercise and Sport, 67,* 13–23.

Marsh, H.W. & Rowe, K.J (1996). The negative effects of school-average ability on academic self-concept – an application of multilevel modelling. *Australian Journal of Education, 40,* 65–87.

Marsh, H.W. & Shavelson, R. (1985). Self-concept: Its multifaceted, hierarchical structure. *Educational Psychologist, 20,* 107–125.

Marsh, H.W., Tracey, D.K. & Craven, R.G. (2006). Multidimensional self-concept structure for pre-adolescents with mild intellectual disabilities: A hybrid multigroup-mimic approach to factorial invariance and latent mean differences. *Educational and Psychological Measurement.*

Marsh, H.W., Trautwein, U., Lüdtke, O., Köller, O. & Baumert, J. (2005). Academic self-concept, interest, grades and standardised test scores: Reciprocal effects models of causal ordering. *Child Development, 76,* 297–416.

Marsh, H.W., Trautwein, U., Lüdtke, O., Köller, O. & Baumert, J. (2006). Integration of multidimensional self-concept and core personality constructs: Construct validation and relations to well-being and achievement. *Journal of Personality, 74(2),* 403–456.

Marsh, H.W. & Yeung, A.S. (1997a). The causal effects of academic self-concept on academic achievement: Structural equation models of longitudinal data. *Journal of Educational Psychology, 89,* 41–54.

Marsh, H.W. & Yeung, A.S. (1997b). Coursework selection: The effects of academic self-concept and achievement. *American Educational Research Journal, 34,* 691–720.

Marsh, H.W. & Yeung, A.S. (1999). The lability of psychological ratings: The chameleon effect in global self-esteem. *Personality and Social Psychology Bulletin, 25,* 49–64.

Marsh, H.W. & Yeung, A.S. (2001). An extension of the internal/external frame of reference model: A response to Bong (1998). *Multivariate Behavioural Research, 36,* 389–420.

Marx, R. & Winne, P.H. (1978). Construct interpretations of three self-concept inventories. *American Educational Research Journal, 15,* 99–108.

Meyer, J.W. (1970). High school effects on college intentions. *American Journal of Sociology, 76,* 59–70.

Möller, J. & Köller, O. (2001). Frame of reference effects following the announcement of exam results. *Contemporary Educational Psychology, 26,* 277–287.

Möller, J., Pohlmann, B., Köller, O. & Marsh, H.W. (2006). *A meta-analytic path analysis of the internal/external frame of reference model of academic achievement and academic self-concept.* Germany: University of Kiel.

Morse, S. & Gergen, K.J.(1970). Social comparison, self-consistency, and the concept of self. *Journal of Personality & Social Psychology, 16,* 148–156.

Muijs, R.D. (1997). Predictors of academic achievement and academic self-concept: A longitudinal perspective. *British Journal of Educational Psychology, 67,* 263–277.

O'Mara, A., Craven, R.G. & Marsh, H.W. (2003). *Evaluating self-concept interventions from a multidimensional perspective: A meta-analysis.* Paper presented at the Joint Meeting of the Australian and New Zealand Associations for Research in Education, Auckland, New Zealand.

O'Mara, A.J., Marsh H.W., Craven, R.G. & Debus, R. (2006). Do self-concept interventions make a difference? A synergistic blend of construct validation and meta-analysis. *Educational Psychologist, 41,* 181–206.

Parada, R. (2006). *Bullying: Intervention, psychosocial determinants and the role of self-concept.* Unpublished PhD Thesis, University of Western Sydney (http://self.uws.edu.au/).

Parada, R., Craven, R.G. & Marsh, H.W. (2003). *The Beyond Bullying Programme: An innovative programme empowering teachers to counteract bullying in schools.* Paper presented at the Joint New Zealand Association for Research in Education and Australian Association for Research in Education conference, Auckland, December.

Parducci, A. (1995). *Happiness, pleasure, and judgment: The contextual theory and its applications.* Mahwah, NJ: Erlbaum.

Pelham, B.W. & Swann, W.B. (1989). From self-conceptions to self-worth: On the sources and structure of global self-esteem. *Journal of Personality and Social Psychology, 57,* 672–680.

Pierce, J.W. & Wardle, J. (1997). Cause and effect beliefs and self-esteem of overweight children. *Journal of Child Psychology Psychiatry, 38,* 645–650.

Robinson, N.M., Zigler, E., & Gallagher, J. J. (2000). Two tails of the normal curve: Similarities and differences in the study of mental retardation and giftedness. *American Psychologist, 55,* 1413–1424.

Rogers, C., Smith, M. & Coleman, J. (1978). Social comparison in the classroom: The relationship between academic achievement and self-concept. *Journal of Educational Psychology, 70,* 50–57.

Rosenberg, M. (1965). *Society and the adolescent child.* Princeton: Princeton University Press.

Schwarzer, R., Jerusalem, J. & Lange, B. (1983). *The change of self-concept with respect to reference groups in school.* Paper presented at the 1983 Annual Meeting of the American Educational Research Association, Montreal.

Segall, M.H., Lonner, W.J. & Berry, J.W. (1998). Cross-cultural psychology as a scholarly discipline: On the flowering of culture in behavioral research. *American Psychologist, 53,* 1101–1110.

Shavelson, R.J. & Bolus, R. (1982). Self-concept: The interplay of theory and methods. *Journal of Educational Psychology, 74,* 3–17.

Shavelson, R.J., Hubner, J.J. & Stanton, G.C. (1976). Validation of construct interpretations. *Review of Educational Research, 46,* 407–441.

Shavelson, R.J. & Marsh, H.W. (1986). On the structure of self-concept. In R. Schwazer (Ed.), *Anxiety and cognitions* (pp.305–330). Mahwah, NJ: Erlbaum.

Sherif, M. & Sherif, C.W. (1969). *Social psychology.* New York: Harper & Row.

Skaalvik, E.M. (1997). Issues in research on self-concept. In M.L. Maehr & P.R. Pintrich (Eds.), *Advances in motivation and achievement* (Vol. 10, pp.51–98). Greenwich, CN: JAI Press.

Skaalvik, E.M. & Hagtvet, K.A. (1990). Academic achievement and self-concept: An analysis of causal predominance in a developmental perspective. *Journal of Personality and Social Psychology, 58,* 292–307.

Skaalvik, E.M. & Rankin, R.J. (1995). A test of the internal/external frame of reference model at different levels of math and verbal self-perception. *American Educational Research Journal, 35,* 161–184.

Skaalvik, E.M. & Valas, H. (1999). Relations among achievement, self-concept, and motivation in mathematics and language arts: A longitudinal study. *The Journal of Experimental Education, 67,* 135–149.

Sommer, K.L. & Baumeister, R.F. (2002). Self-evaluation, persistence, and performance following implicit rejection: The role of trait self-esteem. *Personality & Social Psychology Bulletin, 28,* 926–938.

Sonstroem, R.J. (1997). The physical self-system: A mediator of exercise and self-esteem. In K.R. Fox (Ed.), *The physical self* (pp.3–26). Champaign, IL: Human Kinetics.

Stouffer, S.A., Suchman, E.A., DeVinney, L.C., Star, S.A. & Williams, R.M. (1949). *The American soldier: Adjustments during army life (Vol. 1).* Princeton: Princeton University Press.

Suls, J.M. (1977). Social comparison theory and research: An overview from 1954. In J.M. Suls & R.L. Miller (Eds.), *Social comparison processes: Theoretical and empirical perspectives* (pp.1–20). Washington, DC: Hemisphere.

Suls, J. (Ed.) (1993). *Psychological perspectives on the self (Vol. 4).* Hillsdale, NJ: Erlbaum.

Tiggemann, M. (1992). Body-size dissatisfaction: Individual differences in age and gender, and relationship with self-esteem. *Personality and Individual Differences, 13,* 39–43.

Tracey, D.K. (2002). *Self-concepts of preadolescents with mild intellectual disability: Multidimensionality, measurement and support for the big-fish-little-pond effect.* Unpublished PhD Thesis, University of Western Sydney. (http://self.uws.edu.au/).

Tracey, D.K., Marsh, H.W. & Craven, R.G. (2003). Self-concepts of preadolescent students with mild intellectual disabilities: Issues of measurement and educational placement. In H.W. Marsh, R.G. Craven & D.M. McInerney (Eds.), *International Advances in Self Research* (Vol. 1, pp.203–230). Greenwich, CT: Information Age.

Trautwein, U., Lüdtke, O., Köller, O. & Baumert, J. (2006). Self-esteem, academic self-concept, and achievement: How the learning environment moderates the dynamics of self-concept. *Journal of Personality and Social Psychology, 90*(2), 334–349.

Trautwein, U., Lüdtke, O., Marsh, H.W. & Köller, O. (in press). Tracking, grading, and student motivation: Using group composition and status to predict self-concept and interest in ninth-grade mathematics. *Journal of Educational Psychology.*

Trzesniewski, K.H., Donnellan, M.B., Moffitt, T.E., Robins, R.W., Poulton, R. & Caspi, A. (2006). Low self-esteem during adolescence predicts poor health, criminal behaviour, and limited economic prospects during adulthood. *Developmental Psychology, 42*(2), 381–390.

Upshaw, H.S. (1969). The personal reference scale: An approach to social judgment. In L. Berkowitz (Ed.), *Advances in Experimental Social Psychology, 4,* 315–370.

Valentine, J.C. & DuBois, D.L. (2005). Effects of self-beliefs on academic achievement and vice-versa: Separating the chicken from the egg. In H.W. Marsh, R.G. Craven & D.M. McInerney (Eds.), *International Advances in Self Research* (Vol. 2, pp.53–78), Greenwich, CT: Information Age.

Valentine, J.C., DuBois, D.L. & Cooper, H. (2004). The relations between self-beliefs and academic achievement: A systematic review. *Educational Psychologist, 39,* 111–133.

Vernon, P.E. (1950). *The structure of human abilities.* London: Muethon.

Wells, L.E. & Marwell, G. (1976). *Self-esteem: Its conceptualisation and measurement.* Beverly Hills, CA: Sage Publications.

Wigfield, A. & Karpathian, M. (1991). Who am I and what can I do? Children's self-concepts and motivation in achievement solutions. *Educational Psychologist, 26,* 233-261.

Wylie, R.C. (1974). *The self-concept* (rev. ed., Vol. 1) Lincoln: University of Nebraska Press.

Wylie, R.C. (1979). *The self-concept* (Vol. 2). Lincoln: University of Nebraska Press.

Wylie, R.C. (1989). *Measures of self-concept.* Lincoln: University of Nebraska Press.

Zeidner, M. & Schleyer, E.J. (1999). The big-fish-little-pond effect for academic self-concept, test anxiety and school grades in gifted children. *Contemporary Educational Psychology, 24,* 305–329.